RECLAIMING MY POWER

My Life in the Aftermath of R. Kelly

By

Asante McGee

Copyright © 2020 Asante McGee

All rights reserved.

ISBN: 1734850108
ISBN-13: 978-1-7348501-0-9

DEDICATION

This book is dedicated to the memory of my late grandmother, Julia Lee Carson, who loved me unconditionally and saved me from years of abuse at the hands of my birth mother. I know you did everything you could to protect me and I will never forget that or the fact that you always made me feel loved.

And to the girl I was once was, I want to thank you too. It's because of you that I came to learn and appreciate the pain of my past relationships and because of you that I have learned to love myself again. Thank you for helping me to overcome my fear of saying what I feel and giving me the discernment I need when it comes to trusting others. Because of you, I can now accept my faults and my flaws and start putting ME first above others.

Thank you!
~Asante~

CONTENTS

INTRODUCTION 1

CHAPTER 1 – WHEELS UP 3

CHAPTER 2 – MY MOTHER'S CLOSET 5

CHAPTER 3 – SEAFOOD FRIDAYS 12

CHAPTER 4 – FOREVER CHANGED 19

CHAPTER 5 – HANDSOME YOUNG DEVIL 27

CHAPTER 6 – ME AND UNCLE SAM 36

CHAPTER 7 – CLOSE ENCOUNTERS 50

CHAPTER 8 - DADDY 55

CHAPTER 9 – FLY GIRL 61

CHAPTER 10 – TRAINING DAY 67

CHAPTER 11 – MÉNAGE À TWICE 73

CHAPTER 12 – END OF DAYS 81

    Week 1 81

    Week 2 85

    Week 3 88

CHAPTER 13 – WHEELS DOWN 91

EPILOGUE 94

ACKNOWLEDGEMENTS 98

ABOUT THE AUTHOR 100

INTRODUCTION

Prior to 2017 I had flown under the radar, virtually unrecognized and undetected like an eagle waiting for the perfect moment to swoop down on its prey. Little did I know at the time that I would become the prey instead of the predator. But on that fateful day on July 17, 2017, as I stood there as numb as numb could be, in front of what felt like a million flashing cameras and microphones pointed in my face, I had my "coming out" in the sense that I was able to release the skeleton that had been trapped in the closet for so long. In that moment, that skeleton (me) was allowed to finally speak her truth. Since then, my life has not been the same and hopefully never will be.

When I decided to release my first book , "No Longer Trapped In The Closet, The Asante McGee Story" in 2019, it was under the duress of the public and the networks to get my story out about my relationship with the infamous R. Kelly. They all wanted their portions of the tea and they wanted it poured hot, quick, and plentiful. So, what did I do? I gave it to them and in the process, did a disservice to myself by opening up the door to unimaginable scrutiny under the microscope of the media. I also fell victim to an unforgiving and extremely judgmental public, as well as R. Kelly "trolls" and fans that almost destroyed my family and nearly took me out in the process. Things were so bad for a while that I wanted to end my life! This was exactly what others out there wanted me to do, which for them would have undoubtedly made the story even more salacious.

I've been called everything in the book – stupid, a liar, an opportunist, illiterate, a slut, a whore, and a whole list of things that are far too nasty and painful to repeat. For some reason, people think it's ok to attack me and think I'm not supposed to defend myself. Well, that ends now! This is my time to set the record straight, rebuild my character, and separate myself from the pack. I'm more than just one of the "R. Kelly girls."

I've learned a lot since this whole R. Kelly ordeal started, including that in order to know where you are going, you have to recognize where you've been, no matter how dark and scary those places may be. For me, that part of my story is something that I needed to take a step back, revisit, and now share; not just for my critics and naysayers, but most importantly for those who were or are in similar situations to my own, will read this book, and hopefully be inspired to act.

I've had many low points in my life, especially the day that Rob (R. Kelly) recited a list of rules that included my asking his permission to use the bathroom. In that moment, I found myself not only questioning myself as a grown woman but questioning God. At one point, I even blamed God for everything bad that had ever happened in my life – from my abusive childhood, to my failed family relationships, my bad marriage, and finally the situation with Rob. Why would you save me from two abusive situations only to put me in another one Lord? But in the end, I know now that God's timing is perfect and that He truly makes no mistakes. It took two years for me to see R. Kelly, the monster, instead of Rob, the man I thought I loved and sadly thought loved me too. But now I realize that God used that time to help build the self-respect, self-worth, self-confidence, and self-love that I needed to prepare me for what has become my journey and life's work. I know now that God ultimately wanted me to be that "voice for the voiceless" and to stand up for myself and others in order to Reclaim My Power!

CHAPTER 1 – WHEELS UP

It's September 2019 and as I sit here in a crowded airport surrounded by strangers, crying babies, and the annoying mix of loudspeakers and laughter in my ears; never in my life have I felt so alone. My rose-petal pink nails are freshly dipped and flawless, but the trembling of my outstretched hands is far from that, causing me to wonder how I got to this place.

I bitch at myself in my head saying, "Get it together Sante, what the hell is wrong with you?" I resist the temptation to verbalize my response so that people around me won't think I'm a nut case. Even if I were a nut case, I'd have every right to be, because of everything I've been through. I quickly realize that it's just nerves. After all, I'm on my way to the Emmy Awards, which is something I never imagined in my wildest dreams! Yes, me – Asante – a little dark chocolate girl from the lower 9th ward of New Orleans, will be amongst the stars at the 71st Annual Emmy Awards. But as much as I would like for this to be one of the proudest and most of defining moments in my 40 years of life, it's not. In fact, it's just the opposite. Deep down inside, I'm ashamed because of how all this came about for me.

Around this time six years ago, almost to the day, I had my first "close encounter" on my birthday weekend, with a man who is not only known for being one of the greatest R&B singers of all time – but who has also been described as one of the most devious sexual predators in American history. A year later in January 2014, which was ironically his birthday weekend, we had our first face-to-face encounter, causing life as I knew it then to change forever.

So as I sit here, alone, reflecting on my perceived "arrival" and rise to stardom, I'm also thinking about my departure from the normal life that I always believed God had planned for me. Even though that life included growing up under less-than-favorable circumstances, with a mother who beat the living crap out of me on a daily basis. But as crazy as it sounds, I really wish my mother – my abuser – was here with me now. Yes, sitting right next to me, holding my hand like a normal mother should, telling me "everything's gonna be alright Sante." But in reality, we haven't spoken since 2014 when I saw her in passing at a relative's funeral. She tried her best to avoid eye contact, but I looked her dead in the face.

"Hi Asante."

"Hi Karen," I responded back with no feeling or emotion whatsoever. And that was it. We haven't spoken since. All I know is that she's still alive. She doesn't have my phone number and I don't have hers. As sad as that might sound, I'm okay with it.

I always called my mother by her birth name because in my eyes, she didn't deserve to be called "Mom." I don't know what I ever did to her to make her hate me. I can't help but to think that maybe this moment – my TV Emmy Awards moment – would somehow make her not just like me but make her proud of me too. However, just like other thoughts of my mother, that one quickly dissipates too, as the annoying voice of the lady at the other end of the loudspeaker cuts through my mental musings to announce the boarding of my flight. I quickly spring to my feet, gather my things, and bogart my way into the assembling line of people; all trying to make a mad dash to get to the gate. I'm seated in first class, of course, which is something I've grown accustomed to and something I am learning to believe that I deserve.

Alright, City of Angels, here I come. It's showtime!

CHAPTER 2 – MY MOTHER'S CLOSET

Two Hennesseys, 3 Cokes, and two potty breaks later, it's "wheels down" at LAX. The popping of my ears along with the thumpity-thump of plane wheels hitting the ground are enough to scare the shit out of me and make me say a prayer of thanks for the safe landing at the same time. I power on my phone and am greeted by the buzzing sound of text messages popping one by one onto my cracked phone screen. Somehow, I managed to drop it in Paris during all the commotion of getting surprised by my girlfriends with a pair of mocha brown, size 41 Hermes shoes that nearly took my breath away. That, along with the beauty of the architecture, the culture, and the people of Paris were the highlights of my trip and made my 40th birthday one I'll never forget. It also made me appreciate my life a lot more and how good I really have it now; especially when I think about what everybody, including my family, said I couldn't have or would never be.

Minutes later, I make my way down the breezeway, trying to compose myself quickly. I run my fingers through my shoulder-length Brazilian body wave; resisting the urge to pat it down with the palm of my free hand. My tracks are still tight, and my scalp is still sore, but I rest assured in knowing it will loosen after the stylist flat irons it tomorrow night for the awards. A few minutes later, as I approach the sign marked Baggage Claim, I see a tall, yellow-bone black man wearing a starched white button-down, a Gucci belt, and black Gucci loafers to match standing in the distance. He's holding a white cardboard sign that simply reads MCGEE. *Yep, that's me*, I think to myself, smiling on the inside not only because he's kinda' cute, but also because he's on time, which means I can get a nice nap at the hotel before tonight's shenanigans begin.

"Hi, I'm Asante." I smile politely. He smiles back.

"You have bags you need me to get off the turnstile for you ma'am?"

"Oh yeah," I laugh a little and head toward the baggage claim area.

Thirty minutes later, the tall yellow man, who reminds me of Malcolm X, but without the glasses, opens my door, and grabs my hand allowing me a gentle boost up into the Escalade SUV.

"You never told me your name," I say, as I settle into the plush black leather of the back seat.

"Oh, I'm sorry ma'am," he says in his most professional voice. "My name is Malcolm."

Get the fuck outta here... I think, trying not to smile too hard since he's peeping me through his rearview mirror.

Once again, I'm startled; this time awakened by the slam of a car door. I'm so freakin' tired and discombobulated that I have no concept of time. Before I can pull myself together, a familiar gust of California night air along with Malcolm's outstretched hand greet me through my now open car door.

"Sorry to wake you ma'am, but we're here."

A few minutes later, I make my way up to my room with just enough energy to tip the bellboy, check out the mini bar, and enjoy the view from my penthouse-level suite. From my vantage point, I peep the scene for tomorrow night's event and suddenly the butterflies in my stomach return and my hands start to tremble again. I quickly shake off my nervous jitters, kick off my red bottoms, and peel off my jeans. There's nothing like the smell of clean, cold, luxury, white sheets at the end of a long flight; well, in my case two long flights. From there it's lights out for my third siesta in less than 24 hours.

Once again, the buzz of text messages brings me into full consciousness. *Damn, how long I been sleep?* The digital clock next to my fully lit lamp reads 9:15 pm, indicating that I'm late for my date with a plate of crab legs and crawfish. My next couple of days in L.A. are uneventful for the most part, with the exception of the mishap with my dress, which could have been disastrous and a showstopper for me. In the hustle and bustle of switching hotels to be closer to my designated glam squad, I ended up leaving my dress back at the first hotel. Yes, my original Algernon Johnson design – a dress made just for me for by an up-and-coming designer out of Atlanta, who I'd been stalking on my Insta for months in hopes that he would dress me one day. Welp, it finally happened and ol' boy designed the dress of my dreams – one that every girl dreams of wearing, complete with pink studs, lots of sparkly sequins and a side slit that accentuates my long legs and left thigh.

The softness of the dress reminds me of a more innocent time before all the drama and scandal of my life now, when all I wanted to do was double-dutch jump rope and make mud pies with my cousins from sun-up to sundown, until the streetlights flickered on. It also reminds me of the few good times I had with my mother Karen, mainly on the days that Walter came by to pick us up. As with most of us, my mother had plenty of skeletons in her closet and Walter was one of them. Walter was my mother's lover and my younger sister Carla's father. He was also my on-again-off again father during my younger years. He was always nice to me; definitely nicer than Karen ever was and always treated me like I was one of his own – yes, his own blood child. He even named me, so I've been told. I don't know the whole story, but it was rumored that Walter and Karen met when she was pregnant with me and had a longtime affair through my birth and up until my sister Carla came along six years later. He was never a permanent fixture in our household, but he was around long enough for me to get attached.

I remember the days before my sister was born when Walter would pick me and Karen up to run errands and pay bills. He drove a nice, champagne-gold, tricked out Trans Am and just like I imagined my real father would, Walter always made sure I was strapped in tight in the back seat before we took off. And on the days that were sunny and warm, he took the glass tops off, which always got me excited and made Karen mad because the wind always messed her hair up. My best memories of spending time with Walter were of my head laid back, eyes closed, and the warmth of the Louisiana sun through the open rooftop. Walter and Karen never said much to each other during our long car rides, but every once in a while I'd catch a glimpse from the back of the side of his hand on her thigh or hers on his knee. That was the only true sign of affection I ever saw her give to anyone other than my sister and brothers when they were babies.

But one thing I was thankful for was that Karen never laid a hand on me in Walter's presence; so in a sense, he was like my own personal superhero in that he kept my mother happy and saved me from the beatings – all in a single bound. But every time he left, all bets were off, and she beat me with anything and everything she could get her hands on – from toy BB guns, to wooden boards, to extension cords. The extension cords left permanent welts on me that serve as daily reminders of my strength and the fact that I *am* a survivor in every sense of the word, despite what my critics think. And although my other family members – everybody from my grandmother to my aunts all knew of the abuse I suffered at my mom's hands, I never blamed any of them for not saving me. I truly believe that they did their best to protect me. My grandmother even went as far as to tell her white insurance agent about the abuse, with the hope that the agencies would somehow listen and believe a white man over her, a poor, elderly black woman from the hood, and extend a helping hand. But that didn't happen either.

"We need more evidence," they told him.

"What more evidence do you need?" I remember my grandmother's pleas to him. "Does she need to die first?"

RECLAIMING MY POWER

At that point, I knew no one could help me or save me from my own mother, so for years I endured the abuse until the day I was rescued, but not by Walter this time. I was about ten years old at the time when she sent me to the corner store to buy loose cigarettes. I don't know if it was the mental illness or the demons that caused her to send me, a minor not even of age to wear a training bra, let alone buy cigarettes, to the store.

Two days before, she sent me to my Auntie's house to ask her to pay the light bill. It was ten o'clock at night, pitch black, and I was scared to death. I could've been raped, kidnapped, or worse, but I went out of fear of getting beat down. When I arrived, Aunt Minnie was just as shocked as she was pissed and refused to send me back home. She fed me, bathed me, and sent me to bed with fresh pajamas and a full stomach. The next morning, I ate breakfast with my cousins and was taken to meet my demise in the form of my mother, since Aunt Minnie had to go to work.

I remember the scene as they stood outside, flailed their hands and arms in the air and hurled profanities at each other. They eventually stopped when Aunt Minnie got in her car, slammed the door and drove off with Karen still cursing her out through the rolled-up window. No sooner than my aunt left Karen marched back in the house, instantly grabbed a King knife, and aimed it dead at my chest. I immediately threw my hands up to protect myself from the knife which ended up cutting my right pinky finger almost to the bone. I didn't know I was cut until I saw the blood. My mother obviously panicked at the sight of so much blood, but not enough to take me, her own child, to the hospital. Instead, she created a makeshift bandage and wrapped it up enough to stop the bleeding.

So when I returned home without the cigarettes she sent me for, I knew it would be bad. Before I could get my sentence out, she punched me dead in my right eye with a force so blunt that I lost my balance and fell back. I don't know if it was the shock of being punched or the fear of the next blow that sent me running but I flew out the door, down the stairs, and down the block toward Curran Place, which was the safest haven I knew outside of the protection of Walter. I didn't even realize it until one of the neighborhood kids who stood at the bus stop stopped my full-speed sprint.

"What happened Asante, why you bleeding?" he pointed toward my face.

I slowed my stride enough to make a beeline around their stares and pointing fingers, until I got to Ms. Warren's place. Ms. Warren was affectionately referred to the "candy lady" by all of the neighborhood kids because she always fed us, cleaned us up, and gave us candy – even when our asses were bad and talked back.

"Oh my God! What happened? Who did this to you baby?"

Her words along with the look on her face confirmed my fear – that it just wasn't just hot tears streaming down my face from my eye, but also blood from the blow of my mother's fist. Ms. Warren didn't give it a second thought – she called the police. By the time they got there, Ms. Warren had already cleaned me up, made me a hot washrag compress and fed me. The next knock at the door was from Karen who had come looking for me. Even though the cops were there, I was terrified at the thought that they would send me back home with her to get a matching black eye along with the beating of my life.

Long story short, Karen punched one of the officers and was handcuffed and arrested and thrown in the back of the squad car. When Child Protective Services (CPS) arrived, they took me back to my house to find my younger sister, Carla, who was six at the time; along with my baby brothers Alvin and Kenny. Alvin was one at the time and Kenny who was only two months old. Upon a thorough search, they found everything from BB guns, to wooden boards to extension cords she beat me with almost daily. They even found the King knife she used to damn-near cut my finger off.

The hospital examination confirmed my abuse. The marks on my body, most of which are still with me today, were a dead match with the weapons used against me – from the back of my neck, to my wrists and all down my thighs. We were immediately placed with my grandmother, Grandma Gladys, who was more than happy to take us in. It was January 1990 and for the first time in my young life, I finally felt safe.

CHAPTER 3 – SEAFOOD FRIDAYS

Flawless!! That was the most-used description on all the tweets, posts, and blogs on Emmy night to describe a look that took damn-near 17 man-hours to produce. My dress fit me like a glove, but not just a regular glove, but more like the Michael Jackson, Billie Jean glove – complete with sparkly studs and the whole nine. One look at myself in the full-length hotel mirror wiped away all of the nervous energy I had pinned up over the last couple of days along with the insecurity of nearly 40 years of being told I was too ugly or too skinny or too dark.

Doc's words confirmed it – "Girl, you are snatched! Yasssssss," she squealed and snapped her fingers in the air.

Doc, as everyone calls her is my PR rep, bodyguard, etiquette coach, travel agent, and financial advisor all rolled up into one. Although you can count the years that separate us on one hand, she's like the mother I never had in that she always takes care of me and makes sure that I "go high, even when they go low" – which they often do. I've had my fair share of folks who have loved me then left me, and not just men. Females have despised me since my younger years; most without reason. Countless others have befriended me, in hopes of getting some type of payoff through our associations, only to later betray me and slander my name before getting to fully know me. In fact, I'm still pulling the darts and knives out of my back from some of those petty bitches to this very day.

But I've never had to worry about that with Doc. When she and I first met back in 2018, she didn't want to take me on as a client. I, of course, didn't know that at first, she later confided that little tidbit with me. The drama tied to my name after the fallout from the R. Kelly scandal was reason enough to send my calls to voicemail and my emails to trash. It wasn't about the money or the notoriety because for her, peace was much more precious. I didn't understand it then, but I do now.

At the time we met, the *Surviving R. Kelly* documentary had just been released, which was the perfect time for me to not just build my brand, but to also sanitize my name. I needed a "do-over" and a "fixer" to do some Kerry Washington *Scandal-type* shit. I needed somebody who could rewrite the chapter of my fall from grace and make me look good on paper, in public, and in person. Doc was and has been that person for me. We laugh about it now but we both know that it was our *Nawlins* connection and what she calls "God's divine intervention," that brought us together. Since then, we have cracked crab legs, popped bottles, and crossed seas together and now this – the Emmy's.

Once I finally make it to the end of the red carpet with Doc footsteps away, my feet feel like hooves and my ankles are throbbing just like my heart. My heart is beating out of my chest as I do interview after interview on this carpet that never seems to end. Everywhere I look, I see men in black suits holding clipboards, women in dresses that look like they cost more than I make in a year, and flashing cameras. Lots and lots of flashing cameras. As always, Doc is on point and right on time. She flashes the credentials hanging around her neck at the short man with the slicked-back hair and black Tom Ford-tailored suit, who immediately extends his arm in the direction of the grand ballroom.

I take it all in – from the chandeliers above my head, to the carpet beneath my feet. It's enough to make me pause and take a deep cleansing WHOOSAH breath. Once inside, I see a familiar sight in the distance, just down the long aisle that separates the seated rows on both sides of us. The faceless gold ladies with raised hands and angel-like wings that adorn the stage, look larger than life and a hell of a lot bigger in person than on TV. I quickly snap back to reality when I hear and then spot Danielle's messy ass out the corner of my eye. As we approach, I see Courtney a couple of seats down from her along with Dionne and Cindy. All of them are sitting in the roped off section marked SURVIVING R. KELLEY. I take another deep breath before Doc turns around to do her typical temperature check.

"You all right?"

"Uh huh." I look away, trying to be discreet as I roll my eyes.

"Your good. Come on," she confirms for me, without looking back, as she proceeds to enter the lion's den.

The whispers and evil scowls on the faces of the other R. Kelly girls, as we are often called, are all-too familiar and enough to take me back to a time when my own family considered me the enemy too. It was a few years after my mother, Karen, went to jail for child abuse. Carla, Kenny, Alvin, and I all went to live with my Grandma Gladys. Kenny and Alvin shared the same daddy, who everybody called Stacks, but as much as he used to threaten to beat the hell out of Karen if she ever laid hands on one of his boys, he didn't raise his hand to take either of them when Karen went to prison. Thankfully they were too young to understand and besides, we were safe and out of harm's way living with Grandmama. She was happy to have us there and we were even happier to be there. She took care of us like she gave birth to us herself and showed us the unconditional love that we, as innocents had a right to and deserved.

Without warning and within months, Grandmama's health started to deteriorate. The diabetes started to take control and eventually she lost her eyesight along with daily oversight of us, her "precious grandbabies" as she used to say. With my help as the oldest and most responsible in the household, my mother's younger sister, Aunt Janice, tried her best to be caretaker for Grandmama. She ended up coming to live with us, but without reliable transportation, the trips back and forth across the bridge to the hospital became too heavy of a burden to bear. I tried to help as much as I could by learning to cook and clean and give her insulin when she needed it and I took care of my younger siblings when I needed to, but it wasn't enough. So when my mother's older sister, Aunt Betty offered to help lighten the load, Aunt Janice jumped on the opportunity. But instead of moving on up to a better life and a "piece of the pie," like The Jeffersons did, all we did was move up the map to the state of Mississippi where we got a raw deal and the shortest end of the stick. I was about fourteen or fifteen at the time.

Mississippi may have been a fun state to spell, but it sure as hell wasn't fun to live in. I went from being trusted caretaker and my grandmother's pride and joy, to a burden and black sheep in Aunt Betty's eyes, who always seemed to despise and blame me for putting her sister, my abusive mother, behind bars. The $500 check my grandmama got each month became her payday and I was the meal ticket.

I remember it being like Christmas in July for Karen, but not for me and my younger siblings, when she received the first SSI check for me, which was larger than usual since it was a back payment. She didn't have a driver's license but within days of getting the first check, she was the owner of a new Ford Escort. So when we moved to Mississippi, so did the check – straight into the hands of Aunt Betty, who used it to supplement her shopping habit.

Aunt Betty lived in a house a few blocks away from the house she set me, Grandmama, and my siblings up in after we moved. Her four kids, my cousins, always seemed to have new gear every month around the first of the month, whereas me and my siblings were forced to wear thrift shop and hand-me-downs. I was given a $50 a month allowance to do "whatever I wanted to with it," Aunt Betty said. That "whatever" included my school lunch and snacks, maxi pads, deodorant and any other supplies I needed. She barely kept clothes on our backs or food on the table, so it was a mystery to me where the rest of the money went; especially when you consider that Grandmama always kept our stomachs full and our backs clothed when we were back in NOLA, off of that same $500 check

I missed the big dinners on Sundays, which Grandmama made sure lasted us well into Monday and sometimes even Tuesday. On Wednesdays, we had spaghetti and on Fridays we had seafood. On Saturdays we were on our own, but even then, we never went hungry under Grandmama's watch. In fact, the only time we ever struggled was when her diabetes sent her into the hospital. So the fact that we were back in that same place of vulnerability mixed with so much uncertainty, like we were when Karen was in control, was devastating to me. The last straw was when I asked for a typewriter for my birthday.

"Yeah, you can have one," Aunt Betty said.

I smiled from ear to ear.

"But it'll have to come out of your allowance."

She spoke those words so sweet and as-a-matter-of-factly that you would've swore she was telling me a bedtime story. Then without even making eye contact, she went back to watching her soap operas without giving me a second thought.

Ain't that some shit, I thought, trying to process her words in my teenage brain. *Maxi pads or a typewriter?*

Needless to say, I chose to spend my money on maxi pads because they *weren't* optional, but my dreams of becoming a news reporter at the time were. That day I decided I didn't want to live anymore. In my mind, I couldn't tell which was worse – being straight punched in the face by my own mother, or having my heart ripped out by my own aunt, who was entrusted to love and care for me when my grandmother could no longer. I had become that doormat that no one really noticed, but that always seemed to be in the way. I knew that Aunt Betty blamed me for not only Karen doing the jailtime that she deserved, but she also secretly blamed me for Grandmama getting sick. Eventually, I started to believe that my entire family would be better off and maybe even happier without me. But when the overdose of aspirin didn't take me out of my misery, I did what I thought was the last resort at the time – I went to my school counselor and sang like a bird.

A shift took place that day in my counselor's office that day because I was finally able to transfer everything that had been balled up inside of me for so long – the hurt, the anger, the abandonment – to somebody who seemed to actually care. I knew I couldn't stay in that place anymore and they apparently knew it too because a few days later I was placed in state custody. The fact that Aunt Betty didn't fight for me, confirmed my suspicions about not being loved and apparently served as further justification for having me removed. The day I left my grandma's house and entered into state custody was one of the best days in my life because for the first time in a long time, I had hope. I was numb but I had hope. I felt bad about leaving my little brothers and sister behind and even worse, my grandmama; who was completely helpless and bedridden by then.

I was assigned to a social worker and placed with Ms. Brigman, a nice black lady who also cared for another foster kid. A week into what I thought was finally going to be a "normal life," I was nearly raped by a man who was a guest of my foster sister. If it wasn't for the good Lord, my social worker, and the dirty butcher knife I grabbed out of the kitchen sink to protect myself, the trajectory of my life could've been changed forever that night. And although I spent the rest of my formative years moving from group home to group home, for the first time in a long time, I was happy. I had people that cared about me in the form of my social workers who became like the parents I never had and for the first time in my young life, I actually had friends and a real social life.

My family had always pegged me as being a "fast-ass" and a troublemaker but I was neither. In fact, the one and only time that I had ever been in a fight in my young life was back in third grade when I accidentally cut one of my classmates with a pair of scissors. Naturally, they all assumed I did it on purpose, so my teacher sent me packing straight to the white principal's office, who straight called the police on me. Even the girl's mother knew it was an accident, but my asshole principal insisted on pressing charges. This was my first encounter with the juvenile detention system and was the beginning of a series of encounters with the law for me. I was back on the block before the streetlights came on and an instant celebrity because I had gone to juvie.

While in the group home, I learned a lot about myself and was encouraged to be anything and everything that I could be. My grades were decent, and I was even in the high school band. I played the clarinet, xylophone, and cymbals. I was even in ROTC. Life was finally good – or at least a lot better than it had been for a long time.

It was also during this time that I had my first encounter with the man I've known and affectionately referred to as simply "Rob," who would eventually change my life forever. I was at a group home in Jackson, Mississippi when we were given tickets to go see R. Kelly, Solo, and Escape under the supervision of one of our case workers. Rob and I laughed about it on occasion, sometimes over Hennessy and other times after hot sex, how the first time I saw him was on a stage in front of thousands in a bathtub wearing nothing but white sheer pants and a wifebeater. I was 15 at the time and he was 27.

CHAPTER 4 – FOREVER CHANGED

I became restless about an hour into the Emmy's. The show had definitely lived up to all the hype in terms of glitz and glam, but now I was bored, tired, and hungry. Doc did her best to keep me entertained and where she fell short, my cell phone compensated. *I've got to get this shit fixed pronto.* The dim light illuminated the darkness around me, revealing a series of missed calls and unread texts.

DEVON: What up babygirl?

DEVON: ???

TRINITY: Hey Momma, you look pretty. Love you. Yo son being bad

DOC: I lost you in the shuffle. WYA?

SONYA: Hey girl hey. You cute!!!

DEVON: You must be at the show. Send me some pics.

With a flick of my wrist I did a quick copy and paste of one of the pictures of me on the red carpet that Doc took earlier in the night and sent it to Devon. He didn't deserve it, but I figured, what the hell, I'll make that Negro sweat and regret what he was missing – something he would never have. Apparently he didn't get the memo that we were officially done. It was sent before my trip to Paris. Me and Devon had been cool for years, from the first time I met him at my son's football practice, until his true colors came out. It took a minute for him to step to me and when he did, he came correct in every way. But then he started to show his horns along with his empty pockets once he got too comfortable, I guess. I cooked for him and took care of his kids like they were my own, only for him to cut corners in the worst kind of way.

I should've known something was up when he started taking me to the movies on $2 Tuesdays instead of Fridays and Saturdays like normal folks. But on the day he offered to "go half" on a seafood dinner I planned to cook for him and his kids, I was done. I overlooked him being a functional alcoholic, strike one. Strike two – his cheapness, wasn't as easy to overlook. He didn't get a third strike because after Rob, I was done ignoring red flags when it came to men. I was tired of being treated like an option and decided to run, instead of hide, from men and relationships that I knew in my heart were toxic. I was done being that chick.

DEVON: Damn girl

Just the reaction I wanted, so glad I didn't sex this fool.

Although mere inches separated me from the other four "R. Kelly girls," mounds of bullshit, online arguments, and in some cases, jealousy, made us all-to-familiar strangers. Initially we all seemed to share a sisterhood when we first met and even though we came in all ages, sizes, with different sets of circumstances and attitudes we had one thing in common – at one point in time, we all shared a bed with Robert Sylvester Kelly, known to the world as R. Kelly. And now, tonight, we were collectively being recognized for being survivors of the man who manipulated and abused each and every one of us; some worse than others.

Once the lady with the cute English accent announced our category, which was Outstanding Informational Series or Special, it was as if time stood still. All five of us stood at attention as we sat up in our seats with our beat faces and fitted gowns, waiting to hear the name of the Lifetime documentary we filmed over a year ago. Then we would take the long walk down the red carpet onto the stage, smile for the cameras, maybe hold hands, then go our separate ways.

RECLAIMING MY POWER

One at a time she announced the other series nominated in the category until she finally announced ours – "Surviving R. Kelly." Each announcement was met with cheers and applause; some louder than others, along with an onscreen preview of the work being nominated. It just so happened that my face was the first and only face that showed on the big screen during the preview. I heard screams, hands clapping and whistles from the other girls when the name was first announced, but the minute my face popped up on the screen – crickets.

I couldn't hear exactly what they whispered; nor did I give a damn, but once again, I felt the darts of their hater stares being thrown in my direction. But like the soldier that I am, I didn't break my focus but instead gripped Doc's hand, held my breath and waited. It was so surreal to see my image on the larger than life screen saying the words I so vividly recall saying the day I re-entered the room where I spent some of my loneliest days.

"I don't ever wanna revisit that room again…" Then silence, followed by weak applause.

None of us should've been surprised when they announced Anthony Bourdain as the winner for "Parts Unknown." Despite my disappointment, I couldn't help but feel that if anybody deserved to win, he did. I thought about him and wondered what or how he must've felt at the moment he decided to take his own life. More than likely he felt the same desperation and despair I felt when I, too, attempted to take my own life – not once, not twice, but three times total. Apparently, the third time was *not* quite the charm for me because I'm still here. Thank you Jesus!

Aspirin was my drug of choice the first time but the second time around I opted for something stronger in the form of a bottle of unmarked anxiety pills. I got them from one of my suitemate's nightstand drawer at the group home. True enough, my life was much better being out from under Aunt Betty's control and all her animosity, but something was still missing. I had attended three different high schools across Mississippi from Hattiesburg, to Vicksburg to Jackson. And although I seemed to finally be well-adjusted, I still didn't feel loved.

I know now that one of the things that kept me in the game was the strength harnessed inside of me, even in my weakness, and my love for music. Music was one of the reasons I joined the high school band and one of the things that connected me to Rob (R. Kelly). Back then, if you listened to R. Kelly you were automatically pegged as a fast girl, whereas if you listened to Jodeci, you were halfway romantic. I was never a fast girl, despite what people thought of me; even my own aunts and cousins thought I was having sex when that was the furthest thing from my mind. Regardless, I loved me some R. Kelly and Jodeci. Ironically enough, although I had heard him on the radio before, I was never a fan until I saw him perform onstage, live.

As I neared my eighteenth birthday, I was told that I needed to start the transition into adulthood. In some ways, I already felt like I was an adult. For half of my childhood I took care of and fended for myself. Part of the transition meant being reunited and regular visitation with my family. Eventually I reunited with my grandmother and three siblings, who I had barely seen during the time I bounced around from group home to group home. Although she couldn't see me, she knew I was there, and was happy I was home. I attended mandated therapy sessions, which was helpful and seemed to get along much better with Aunt Betty this time around. Long story short, I managed to get through my senior year and in the blink of an eye, my graduation day came and went.

Karen had been released from jail by that time, but didn't attend, nor did any of her sisters, including Aunt Betty. A couple of my great aunts from back home attended. Honestly, I couldn't care less, since the only person I loved and who I knew loved me was Grandmama. That's why losing her was and still is one of the hardest things I've ever had to endure. Out of everyone in my family, I knew that my grandmama loved me without a doubt. Secretly, I knew that some of them despised me because of how hard my grandmama loved me.

RECLAIMING MY POWER

I had to find out from a neighbor that Grandmama had passed. I was less than a hop, skip, and a jump away from home at Pearl River Community College, but nobody bothered to come by or call and tell me that she died. Karen attended the funeral, but we barely said two words to each other. She didn't acknowledge me as her daughter and I damn sure didn't acknowledge her as my mother. I hadn't seen her since the day she stared me down from the back of the squad car as they took her away in hand cuffs. She had the same crazy look in her eyes, but now that I was older I knew that she truly was certifiably crazy.

With Grandmama dead, I became completely disconnected from my family. My brothers and sister were older and seemed to be fine on their own; besides Grandmama was the glue that kept us together. Life as I knew it had ended. Again. And just like the day I left to enter foster care I was numb. At 19, I was alone and lonely. I had a guy friend that I didn't really consider a love interest at the time. That quickly changed when I got pregnant.

I met Gary when I was in high school through one of my friends. It took a while for him to grow on me. He always came through dressed in dirty work clothes and although he was only four years my senior, he looked a lot older than he really was. He had a kid already, which was a strike for me, plus I suspected he was a drug dealer since he changed cars like he changed clothes. Two strikes. He was there for me when my grandmother passed and became like family to me. After she passed, me and Aunt Betty were at each other throats about everything. Even though I was legally an adult and lived in the dorm, she did her best to control me and I felt like she tried to turn my own siblings, the only real family I had left, against me.

It was one of those times that we were "into it" when Gary came through like Calgon, to take me away. He took me to a hotel instead of my dorm that night, where we had sex for the first time. I wish I could say it was memorable, but it wasn't. But will I always remember it? Yes, because my life was forever changed that night.

It didn't take long for the symptoms to appear. I was always tired – I went to class, came home, went to sleep, woke up, went to class, came home and went back to sleep. A few of my dorm buddies teased me – one of them said, "your eyes are shining, I think you're pregnant."

"Nahhhh." I dismissed it like it like I did my period when it didn't come.

Finally, I ended up at the campus clinic where they confirmed my unspoken suspicions and my worst nightmare that I was pregnant. My roommate was the only soul I told. There was no reason to tell Gary since abortion was my only choice. But the night I woke up in a cold sweat after a dream where I died on the operating table, I knew it was a sign from God. That dream cemented my decision to keep my baby; which, in retrospect, was one of the best decisions I ever made in life.

It took a while for me to tell anybody, let alone Gary. For weeks I avoided him like the plague and wore big, baggy, potato-sack clothes. I was skinny but my boobs were already big, so it was easy for me to hide it. My family had always accused me of being a "fast ass" even though I was far from it. While other girls my age were out hunting dick and money, I was looking for love. Gary was the first guy that ever showed me any love – he spent time with me, talked to me, listened to me and tried his best to hold me down financially too. All those actions for me, equated to love. And while I don't think I ever fell in love with him, because of some of his ways and actions, I had a lot of respect for him and trusted him enough to give him my virginity.

I told him by accident on the phone in one of our heated conversations that I was pregnant.

"…that's why you gonna' be paying child support!!!"

"Huh?"

RECLAIMING MY POWER

"Yeah, mutha-fucka, I'm pregnant!"

I got through my 8th month undetected until one of my friends tried to surprise me with a baby shower. Gary, Aunt Betty and the few friends I had were all invited, but none of them showed up.

The night before I went into labor, I had a dream that I died. The next day I woke up to a stomach tight as a basketball that seemed to pulsate on and off like a beating heart. I had no idea what was happening and was a little scared since I didn't feel the baby move as much. Keep in mind, I was oblivious to most female things since I never had the blessing of having "the talks" that most young girls were afforded – I didn't know what a period was until the blood started flowing, I didn't know about the birds and the bees until I watched a porno with one of the group home girls one night, and I definitely didn't know what to expect when expecting. So pretty much everything I learned was learned by trial and error.

By the time I had Trinity, I had my own place and a car that I got with the help of the federal government in the form of a much-needed income tax check. Between Gary and my old roomie, I was barely ever alone. It was mid-afternoon by the time I got comfortable again. I ate one of my favorite meals – barbecue chicken, mac and cheese, and sweet peas. It put me back to sleep and by the time I woke up around 5:30 that evening, I was in full blown labor.

Trinity was born on July 22, 1999. My labor was pretty uneventful and painless after they gave me an epidural. I figured Karen beat me so much that I had a high tolerance for pain, which helped that much more.

We hung in there as long as we could, but eventually the arguments got worse and the space between me and Gary grew. The nail in the coffin was when he got another chick pregnant. And not just any chick, but a 16-year-old chick, which was strike three. I was done with him. I ordered a blood test blood test to seal the deal. It earned me a measly $128 a month child support. It wasn't much, but it helped along with the money I saved up from working at Popeye's, to get me back to New Orleans.

Trinity was about a year old when I took the plunge, packed up everything I had, and moved back to the place where it all started, New Orleans. I hoped that I could create a fresh start for me and my baby, and maybe even reconcile with my family there. I moved in with a friend, her mother, and grandmother who agreed that me and my baby could stay there until I got on my feet.

A year later, I found myself living in my car with a one-year-old, a pocket full of food stamps, and no one to turn to.

CHAPTER 5 – HANDSOME YOUNG DEVIL

The disappointment of being amongst the night's "biggest losers" didn't set well with the other ladies – they all bounced and so did we. The realization didn't set in for me until the walk across the theater complex to the Governor's Ball. I was disappointed but also felt relieved. The anticipation was over and now it was time to face reality and move on. *Now go get your shit together and be great Sante!* It was a full circle moment in the sense that the same peace I felt when I first arrived in L.A. to film the first docuseries was similar to the peace I felt now.

My initial sense of peace came when I was able to sit down and purge all of the dirty details and emotions of my time with R. Kelly after being told repeatedly by the world: *You're overexaggerating! No one will believe you! You're a grown woman so you knew better! Why didn't you leave sooner?* People unfairly judged me without knowing or even wanting to know the truth. They based everything off of the blogs, TMZ, YouTube, and social media. The opportunity with Lifetime not only gave me the opportunity to share my story with the world and attempt to clear my name, but it also gave me the hope of joining forces with other women who shared similar experiences. It also gave me a sense of sisterhood and support that I lacked and yet longed for, for a very long time. And although in the long-run I was sold a pipe dream, I don't regret the experience. Not one bit.

Now that I was at a crossroads, the hype had faded fast – no more related appearances, no more glamourous award shows and Rob was finally headed to jail. America and the world had moved on in search of the next big scandal they could sink their teeth into. The peace was intoxicating knowing that the drama associated with Rob and his "girls" was all in my rearview mirror. I could officially move on to the next bigger and better chapter of my life, which included building my brand, expanding my business, and stacking my paper.

Once we made it over to the Governor's Ball, we were greeted again by men dressed in black with clipboards and headsets and a hell of a buffet. Doc and I both were starved so we wasted no time – we found our table and headed straight for the buffet line. Along the way I spotted Anthony Anderson, who I had always loved even before *Black-ish*. He was/is one of my favorite comedians and actors and my homeboy, in my head of course. Although meeting celebrities was now par for the course for me, I was a little starstruck when I saw him. I knew I had to meet him and take a picture too!

"Ooooooh Doc, there go Anthony Anderson, I need a picture!"

"Wait fool, let me go talk to him. Get ready."

Obviously she was a fan too, but she kept it together as she casually walked over to him like she was going to check the mail.

"What's up Anthony?" She smiled and giggled at the same time.

"What up lady?" He smiled.

You would've thought they were old friends the way they whispered and laughed and chatted it up for the next five to ten minutes, while I stood there invisible and starving. I stood back for a minute and let them do their thing. The music was loud, but my growling stomach was louder. I looked toward the buffet, around the room, which was filling up fast and then back at Doc. She and Anthony both looked at me like they were up to no good. Then out of nowhere he blurted out, "she's a grown ass woman, if she wanna take a picture, she need to ask herself."

I was cold-busted.

"Can I have a picture with you Mr. Anthony?" I laughed.

"Now that's what the hell I'm talking about," he said, revealing his signature smile.

"I'm Asante."

"I know who you are, now come on here girl and get this picture."

I introduced myself and the three of us made small talk for a few more minutes before we finished our trek to the buffet. He was cool…real cool.

A couple of hours and several photo ops later, we were full, sleepy, and more than ready to go. I was thankful for not only a great night that didn't start out so great, but also for the blessing of having this fine man assigned to us for the entire weekend.

I clocked the ride at just under 20 minutes, but it felt more like 45. Doc ran down everything I missed throughout the course of the night, specifically the shit the other girls talked about me when they thought she wasn't listening. Her lips moved but it was almost like she was on mute, because I didn't hear a word of it. I really wasn't trying to hear it because I was at that place where I simply didn't care anymore. The drama of the past few years had finally taken its toll on me and I was ready to get back to Atlanta and on with my life. This trip marked the beginning of the end for me and a new beginning, just like the one I planned for myself and my baby Trinity back when I returned to New Orleans from Mississippi in the summer of 2001.

Pre-Katrina New Orleans was just like I remembered it years ago and I was glad to be home. I missed the culture, the people, and the po boy sandwiches; especially Banks Po Boys. Trinity and I ended up staying with a friend, her mother, and grandmother. Aside from the monthly child support I received off and on, I had virtually no contact with Gary and I was cool with that. I missed the companionship of a man and wanted Trinity to have a relationship with him as she got older, but I need the time and the space to heal first. So when I met a guy named Ramey at the club one night, I fed him with a long-handled spoon. I was determined not to let another man get close to me. Ever! I don't know what it was about me and so-called "bad boys" but back then it I was a magnet for drug dealers and babymakers.

Ramey was different from Gary in a lot of ways, but he was also downright disrespectful and violent, which could've cost me my life. We eventually ended up getting an apartment together in the 5th Ward where he paid all the bills. On the night he got picked up for a probation violation, which landed him in jail. Instead of going with my gut, packing up my shit and leaving with my baby, I stayed and waited for him while he served time.

The money he left didn't last long, especially since we had moved away from the wards where my cousin lived, which meant I had no childcare and no job either. He got out and went back to slinging dope again. The burnt spoons I used to find in the kitchen should have been a dead giveaway that he was using, but I continued to turn a blind eye.

The day he first laid hands on me, I was in the kitchen and had just finished feeding Trinity. I don't remember what we argued about that day – we argued daily – but he hit me so hard that I fell into the refrigerator and folded onto the cheap linoleum tile like a ragdoll. At least with Karen, I always saw the blows coming. This one was totally out of the blue and was the first time I had ever been hit by a man; or should I say a male, since *real* men don't lay hands on women. She was too young to understand, but the look of confusion and fear on my baby's face was one that I'll never forget and enough to make me pack up all my shit and leave the same day.

I ended up back in transitional housing and back on food stamps, but we were safe and that's all that mattered. I was able to find work again but with no transportation and no childcare I had to take the bus and work doubles to make ends meet. I was too proud but too ashamed to call my aunties. Number one – I knew they would talk about me like a dog and number two – I knew they didn't have the means to help themselves, so how in the hell were they supposed to help me? I told the nice case worker at the food stamp office about my situation and that I had nowhere to go so she made a couple of phone calls and found me transitional housing. The program allowed women ages eighteen to twenty-two with children a place to stay for up to two years.

It was there at Liberty House where I learned basic living skills, like interviewing for a job, saving money, and finding housing. I had to provide my own essentials like towels, soap, toothpaste, and diapers for my baby. Shortly after I arrived, I connected with one of my cousins who came to visit but didn't offer to me a place to stay. Although I was given two years to stay, I gave myself six months. I was determined to get back on my feet! I not only had a daughter who was depending on me to take care of her, but I had also made up my mind that I didn't travel that far to fail.

Ramey eventually found me and talked me into letting him visit. The bastard tried to rough me up right there in the transitional house. I heard my grandmother's voice just as clear as day saying, *if a man ever hits you baby, you slice his thing off and put it on a platter and hand it back to him.* But because the sight of blood makes me nauseous, that wasn't an option. I truly wanted to kill him but instead I had him thrown out and a restraining order put on him. Good riddance!

By God's grace, I got a job at Harrah's Casino as a slot attendant which allowed me to meet my expenses and save some money. Eventually I saved enough and was able to move out of Liberty House and into a unit in New Orleans infamous Fifth Ward projects. One of my aunts lived down the block, which worked out in my favor since she was able to watch Trinity while I worked over night and I returned the favor by keeping her baby during the day.

Once again, I was in that *I'm done with men* mode. But that didn't last for long. I was in transitional housing for about another year and a half. Me and Cassie, one of the other girls who had been there just as long as I had, decided to get a house together. It was around the time of New Orleans' second biggest celebration next to Mardi Gras – Essence Festival. Me and Cassie were headed back to our house from the coliseum when a dude swooped up on me and grabbed my hand. I immediately snatched it back.

"Negro I don't know you!"

"But I wanna know you. My name is Henry."

I didn't give him the privilege of eye contact or conversation; but instead walked faster and tried my best to ignore him. In the meantime, his homeboy made his moves on Cassie. Long story short, they ended up giving us a ride home, which was just a couple of blocks away. Henry had jokes, which I liked. When we got back to our place, me and Henry sat on the porch and talked while Cassie and his homeboy stood on the curb by the car chatting it up. When he mentioned he had to pee, without hesitation, I pointed my finger in the direction of the side of the house.

"I don't know you like that to let you in my house. You better whip that thing out and pee around the corner."

We both laughed.

As much as I hate to admit it now, Henry was a handsome young devil, and *the devil* was exactly what he turned out to be in my life. He was mid-height for me; about 5'6 or 5'7, with an athletic build, light-skinned, and curly hair; a dead-ringer for the singer Ginuwine. He was fine. Period. And although I wasn't into yellow dudes, he had a way about him that made me feel comfortable, desired and eventually loved.

The next day, me and Cassie were outside on the porch and noticed a car that resembled Henry' car from the night before, a black Galant, to be exact. I went inside to get my cell phone from the charger and noticed several missed calls from, guess who? Henry.

"Hey shorty, I was in the area so thought I'd stop by."

I didn't believe him but went with it. When he asked to take me out, I snapped back with, "if you take me out, you gotta take my daughter out too."

"That's cool, we must be going to McDonald's then." He laughed, which made me laugh.

I lived in the Fifth Ward at the time and he lived in New Orleans East, which were about 15 minutes in opposites direction from one another. Our relationship moved fast and like typical relationships we spent most of our time on the phone, making small talk and getting to know each other better. So when he invited me to his house, I knew he wanted to seal the deal and I wasn't surprised. I found out later that he shared the house with his girlfriend, who happened to be in the hospital at the time giving birth to his baby. *Go figure.*

I was thankful that I didn't let my emotions and physical urges get the best of me right away. Was I attracted to him? Hell yeah. But was I ready to take our relationship to the next level and give him the jewels? Hell no. Especially since at I had three other guys I saw at the time. There was Ralph, who was an older guy and manager at a local burger joint and Frank who was a police officer. They were both good dudes and good to me and my daughter. I liked both of them for different reasons, but not enough to give my body to either of them. The beauty of it is that they all knew of each other – minus names and details of my relationship with each. This type of transparency allowed me to avoid the drama and confusion and maintain a clear conscious. But in the long-run, Henry won the prize. I cut Frank and Ralph off without a second thought.

Nearly a year after we met and after numerous sexual encounters, mostly to R. Kelly music, Henry and I took the plunge and moved in together. I got pregnant shortly after that. *Damn.*

I knew I wasn't ready for another kid, which is why I held my ground and maintained celibacy until I felt the time was right. A year later, I moved in with him and got pregnant not too long after. I wasn't ready for another kid, but in the heat of the moment, I foolishly relied on the pull-out method to get the satisfaction we both wanted instead of the protection we both needed. Pre-ejaculation is real – I am a witness, twice over.

The first red flag came when I was six months into the pregnancy when I had my first encounter with the other woman, who happened to be the same woman he was living with when he met me. Not to mention, the mother of his fifth child. Somehow Henry coaxed her into giving me a ride from the dealership after I dropped my car off for servicing. Our conversation started out casually enough with small talk and uncomfortable pleasantries. I was uncomfortable given the fact that I was now with and shared a home with the father of her child. And that I was about to have his baby. But it was more than that.

I don't specifically recall what we were discussing when the topic came up, but what I do recall quickly correcting her with, "No, this is Henry's baby."

A few hours later, I found myself in the lion's den with two of the three other women Henry was fucking. He had told them that I was his roommate and that another guy had gotten me pregnant, so he was staying there to *help me out*. *Unfuckingbelievable*. I sat there, on the couch in the living room that Henry and I shared. I rubbed my bulging belly, nonchalantly stroked my hair and said very little. Instead, I watched and listened as they bumped their gums and as they each gave their own versions of their individual relationships with the father of my child. My version was simple – we met, moved in, screwed, and were now having a baby together. He took good care of me and my daughter and made me laugh. That was it. I honestly couldn't say I was in love with him or that we had big plans other than just doing life together. Considering all that I had been through up to that point, I was just there, along for the ride and enjoyed the sense of stability Henry provided. That was it.

Together, they tried to convince me that he was no good and that I should leave him alone. In the back of my mind, I knew I had to leave. When Henry got word through one his girls of the lynch mob waiting for him at the house, he snuck in through a back window and ear hustled as long as he could before he stormed into the living room like a bat out of hell cussing and fussing and calling us all out of our names.

By the time everyone had calmed down and cooler heads prevailed, Henry was given the ultimate ultimatum. Not by me, but by Keisha and Danesha.

"So what you gonna do Nigga? You need to choose."

All eyes were on Henry. I was numb and honestly didn't care one way or another. I was used to being the underdog and the low man on the totem pole, so I was prepared to cut my losses, have my baby, and move on like I always did.

He didn't flinch or stutter when he walked over to where I stood in the corner of the room, put his hand on my stomach and said, "I'm stayin' right here with my baby."

The look on their faces matched the look on mine. I was in just as much shock as they were that he chose me.

"Well I'm still gonna fuck him," Danesha popped off, grabbed her purse and stormed out, slamming the screen door behind her.

She made good on her promise too.

CHAPTER 6 – ME AND UNCLE SAM

Months passed without incident. I gave birth to Little Henry (Junior) on July 31, 2003. I worked temp jobs to make ends meet while Henry sold dime bags and worked at Soul Train Fashion, which was and still remains a staple in New Orleans. He stayed gone a lot, but always came back with money in hand and since the bills were always paid on time, I rarely complained. To me, he was the life vest that helped me to stay afloat, but all the while he was the one drilling holes in a ship that would eventually sink. I thought I was in love with him by that time. I took temp work when money was tight, but for the most part I spent my days taking care of my babies, cooking and cleaning.

Rob had come out with his hit "Ignition" around that time, which became one of many of his hits in my growing rotation of R. Kelly favorites. I spent my days back then on the living room couch watching him along with my other R&B favorites do their thing on BET. In spite of the rumors and allegations against him, I was still a fan. I remember when the first sex tape came out, that allegedly showed him with an underage girl. That was followed by other allegations of Rob forcing himself onto another underage girl. But because the charges never stuck, I, like a lot of his *true* fans, stood behind him and continued to support him by buying his music and helping him to sell out arenas worldwide. Yes, I was that chick that would put you out of my house if you even so much as uttered one negative word about R. Kelly.

My world was quite different from his back then and still is. Henry made me feel as if I had an easy life, sprinkled with a sense of family, which I never had prior to this. Along with his ability to make me laugh – even when I was mad – all of this made it easy to fall for him and even easier for me to stay, despite his lies and love of other women.

Although I had long given up on being a pediatrician and a news reporter, my dream of joining the military so that I could travel the world, learn new languages, and serve my country, never left me. I enjoyed ROTC in high school and saw myself in a career that offered stability and a good income since I knew early on that college and a regular 9 to 5 wouldn't be my path. Upon my return to NOLA from Mississippi and months before I met Henry, I contacted an Army recruiter about joining only to be told that I didn't qualify since I was a single mother. So when asked me to marry him, it seemed like a no-brainer to marry and travel the world with the father of my child. It wasn't a fancy proposal; in fact, it wasn't a proposal at all. He woke up one morning, and simply said "let's get married."

"Ok."

And just like that, we were off to the courthouse to file for a marriage license. During the 24-hour waiting period, we went to Kay Jewelers where I picked out a ring that wasn't my first choice, but one that he said he could afford. I later traded it in for my ring of choice. Two days later on January 26, 2004, Henry and I were married. It wasn't the happiest day of my life, but close enough. It marked the start of me taking my life back and in some ways my power too, because it meant that I could now enlist in the military.

Apparently, Uncle Sam wanted me, and I wanted him too – more than ever. I started a long process of paperwork and a stressful testing period. There was the ASVAB test along with a whole bunch of other tests I had to pass first. Once I passed those, I had to take a PT test, which I also passed. For the first time in a long time, I was excited about my life and determined to make a fresh start for me and my family. Our plans were full-proof, or so I thought. So when the call came that Henry had gotten arrested, it fucked everything up. My first thought was *damn, here we go*. I assumed that he had been busted for slinging drugs, but it was nothing like that. Come to find out, he kicked the door down at Danesha's house after he got word that she had been screwing another dude in the presence of his daughter. He was charged with some type of invasion or trespassing charge, which meant more money out of our household. My dumb ass didn't know he still dealt with Danesha – I later found out that he never stopped. I couldn't be mad at anyone but myself – after all, she forewarned me when she told me straight up, "I'm still gonna fuck him."

The night she showed up at our apartment confirmed it for me. I was on my way to the laundromat downstairs on the other side of the complex when Henry called to tell me he had to meet Danesha to pick up his daughter. So when I spotted her car as it circled the parking lot of the complex as if she was doing surveillance, I was confused as hell but knew in my gut that shit was about to get ugly. I couldn't dial Henry's digits fast enough but by the time he finally picked up, we were both already out of our cars and she was in my face calling me all types of *dumb bitches* and telling me how stupid and dumb I was for staying with him.

One thing led to another and not only did we get into a physical altercation, but I hit her car after she blocked me in when I tried to leave. By the time Henry got there, it was too late. By that time, we had already exchanged plenty of blows, insults and profanities. Long story short, Henry and I both went to jail that night; me for a bogus charge of Stalking and him for Intimidating a Witness. How in the hell did I stalk her when she came to where I lived? That charge was beyond me, but because Henry had a prior charge, I was guilty by association. Also, from the looks of things when the police finally arrived, I played a solo game of bumper cars with her car. I don't know if it was her nerve in invading my home space that caused me to black out in a fit of rage, or the knowledge of her and Henry still messing around right underneath my nose, but that night marked a turning point for me. I had stooped to a whole new level in that it took me back to a time and a place that I never wanted to revisit – the third grade when I was detained for something that wasn't my fault.

This was the beginning of my criminal track record for incidents where I considered myself as collateral damage.

I was arrested and booked that night and actually spent the night in jail but was out the next morning. Henry worked through one of his homeboys to bail me out, even before he got out. Once we bailed out, we made moves like Bonnie & Clyde which included a change of address. As sad as it sounds, I was more concerned about jeopardizing my future in the military than I was about if Henry truly was cheating with Danesha. We both knew that we needed to move and start fresh in a new location in order to avoid any interaction or confrontation with the "baby mama." Period! We were in the clear for the time being, but our new future was still at risk. I had two choices – either wait for a long, ugly trial or plead no contest, pay a hefty fine and save my future. Needless to say, I chose what was behind door number two – the fine.

With all the court costs and bail we had accumulated we were tapped out so we didn't have the money to pay it. My enlisting sergeant was a nice and solid guy that kept his promise to do everything in his power to get me in. He not only went to bat for me when my background check came back dirty, but also fronted me the money for the fine. He became like the church tithes I never could commit to back then. Every 1st and 15th when I got paid, so did he.

In December of 2004, I was sworn in and took an oath that was more solemn and solid to me than my wedding vows – an oath to serve my country proudly. A few days later, I was off to basic training in Fort Jackson, South Carolina, on the first flight that I had taken in my 24 years of life. It was a fear that I quickly conquered once I got past take-off. I don't remember if Rob told me or if I heard it from somebody else that he was afraid to fly. Thinking back on my very first flight, I can only assume that it was the brutal and bumpy takeoff that made him so uneasy. It was my first of many flights to come.

My basic training experience was just like in the movies – hard as hell! But because I was born and raised tough, I knew I was made for this. Second to being away from my kids, I would say that the hardest part of basic training for me was having to consume those nasty MREs. Me being a picky eater didn't help, but because I was the "spoiled one" in our group, I had my pick of the litter when it was MRE time. My "favorites", if you could call them that, were the Peanut Butter and Chilli Mac MREs, which became my meals of choice. I was also blessed to have the what I considered to be the coolest male drill sergeants on the planet. They not only spoiled me by turning a blind eye on a lot of mischievous shit I did, but they also collectively made up for the female drill sergeants that always tried to go extra hard. I guess like a lot of us who are female, or of color or in positions of authority – or sometimes a combination of all three – they felt the need to go the extra mile to prove themselves, even at the risk of being labeled bitches.

Another one of my pain points while in basic was the wilderness. Throughout the course of 12 long, hard, and lonely weeks, we were required to spend 3-4 days in the woods. This meant, in addition to eating nasty MREs, that we had to also use porta-potties. I can truly say that the experience was designed to show you what you were made of and at the same time prepare you for war. I remember getting up extra early in the morning to handle my business in the porta-potties because #1 I wanted my privacy and #2, it was hard to stomach taking a shit on top of everybody else's shit. I made the best of my situation regardless and on the nights that I was assigned to keep watch, sometimes in the rain and freezing cold, I usually talked to Henry or listened to music, to pass the time.

Ironically, Rob's *Happy People* album was out around that time; but based on his increasing legal issues, I'm quite sure he was far from happy back then. Neither was I. You might be wondering how did I talk to Henry during Basic? Because I was a rule-breaker, I smuggled my cell phone into the barracks, which always helped to keep my spirits up and in touch with reality. But my reality was that I was miles away from home and estranged from my extended family, which included my everyone from my biological mother to my aunts and even my siblings. Aside from the occasional phone call or text message, I was pretty much the black sheep of the family. I secretly wondered if any of them would be proud of me and the fact that I had gone off to make something of my life by getting married, starting a *real* family, and establishing an honorable career. But the lack of communication and concern confirmed my suspicions that they could probably care less. As painful as it was, it became and still is my reality.

Meeting my "bestie," Kala Smith, or "Smith" as I later came to know her and refer to her as, was undoubtedly the best part of my entire experience of basic training. She has remained my best friend, confidant, and "ride or die" to this very day. We don't see each other nearly enough, but when we do speak or get together, it is as if we never skipped a beat – me and Smith can literally talk for hours. The formation of our friendship was rocky at first, to say the least. We saw each other almost every day for the first couple of weeks of Basic, but never spoke. She was always the quiet one whereas I was always the quiet storm. I have to admit that I had the best of both worlds back then; especially when it came time to take my weekend passes once I graduated from basic training into AIT. Why? Because I got time away from the barracks and conjugal visits with my husband. Whereas a lot of the ladies used their time away to frequent the local night clubs and bars in search of dick, I had dick that came to me, in the form of my husband Henry. Although his visits were few and far between, I enjoyed the time with him; sometimes too much.

After graduation from basic training I was off to AIT, which is short for Advanced Individual Training. Halfway through my training there, Henry was allowed to visit. During one of his visits, although I had a pass, I was told I couldn't leave base for some bullshit one of the other girls did. Because I was guilty by association, they told me I couldn't leave. Being the rebel that I was, I left anyway and was declared AWOL, (absent without leave) the next morning. It took Henry's lies, pleas to my drill sergeant, Commanding officers, and ultimately God's favor, to get me off the hook.

I had much more fun, food, and freedom at AIT. The icing on the cake was that Smith (Kala) was also there. The 9 weeks I spent in AIT paled in comparison to my 12 weeks of basic training in terms of positive experiences. Not only did AIT prepare me for my career of choice but was also the place where I was introduced to the best Chinese food this side of heaven. Dinner was from 4 to 5 pm each day and lights out was at 9 pm. So by the time 8 o'clock came around, we were usually starving, but made fast friends with the local Chinese delivery man, who hooked us up with undercover deliveries almost nightly.

In addition to the bomb Chinese food, another luxury of AIT were the weekend passes. During one of my pass weekends, I remember getting caught coming back late. I was terrified of being late – I was running, breathing all hard, trying my best to make it into formation without getting busted. Smith, on the other hand, knew she would be late from her pass, but the difference was that she didn't give a shit. Instead, she walked in and got into formation without a care in the world and neither of us ended up getting busted. We laugh about that shit to this very day.

At Ft. Lee, I was in training to become a 92 Foxtrot, also known as a petroleum specialist, where my responsibility would be to gas up the helicopters and trucks for combat. Sadly enough, I never got to fulfill the role but instead did mostly clerical work at my next duty station. I was assigned to the Infantry unit and remained a part of it for my four years of service. Being a part of that unit came with its prestige and risks because it meant that that I was on the list to ship out to war if the opportunity came up. Prior to finishing basic training, we were asked to provide a wish list of the duty stations we wanted to ship out to after AIT. Call it karma, but Fort Drum, New York was at the bottom of my list, but apparently at the top of theirs, because that's where I ended up.

Scary, dreary, and lonely are the best words I can use to describe my arrival at Fort Drum. When I arrived in 2005, I didn't know what to expect and didn't care because I knew my family would be reunited....finally. I stayed in the barracks until I found off-post housing, while waiting to get the golden ticket, in the form of on-post military housing. I didn't mind living off-post because the Army paid all of my expenses, with the exception of my cable and internet bills, which I didn't mind paying. Besides, Henry and the kids took the first thing smoking out of New Orleans and for the first time in a long time, I felt a sense of normalcy and hope for the future. I had a good job, good income, beautiful kids and an unfaithful husband – the unfaithful husband part was something I didn't sign up for.

Henry wasted no time. Within days after his arrival in New York, he managed to hit all of the local hot spots, on and off post. Even though they were still young, it was still an adjustment for the kids to be reunited with me and with each other. You see, for the 12 weeks I was in basic training and AIT, Trinity stayed with the mother of one of my best friends; who I trusted with my life and hers while Lil' Henry stayed with his father. They went from living in damn-near poverty to living in the lap of luxury where membership had its privileges. Everything about our lives now were nice, very nice. But within weeks after his arrival, Henry's name was in the streets and my reputation was ruined in a matter of months as the wife of a philandering dependent. Co-workers knew my husband, including one of my battle buddies, who I later found out he had a brief fling with.

"Hello?"

"Yes?"

"Who is this?"

"It depends, who is this?"

"This is Henry's wife, now who the fuck is this?!"

"It's me, Dana, Asante."

"Damn Dana. Really? I'm really just trying to figure out, why are you all up in my husband's phone."

"You know me Sante, I didn't mean for this to happen. But one thing led to another and…."

You know the rest. This same dialogue became the story of my life and a template for many conversations with the "other women" that were to follow in my 13 years of marriage.

Just prior to Hurricane Katrina hitting New Orleans, in what was to be the most catastrophic hurricane in history, I got the call that my youngest brother had been shot after getting into an argument with one of the girls in the neighborhood. He had severe liver damage, so it didn't look good, but meant that I got a two-week pass to go back home to New Orleans to check on him. During the short time I was there, I realized how much I missed it. Once again, I was taken by the color, the culture, and the food. I missed the freedom the streets offered, which was far from the structure that came with military living.

Once Katrina hit, home was never the same. The storms hit hard but the devastation of losing people I grew up with and some family, who were forced to move, was much harder. The folks who didn't have the finances or will to stay and rebuild were forced out and replaced by mostly rich white people who did. The house I grew up in which sat in the area between the 9th Ward and the Florida Projects, was completely ripped away and the neighborhood looked nothing like I remember growing up. Nothing was ever the same again and like a lot of NOLA natives, I vowed to never return to live there.

A few months after my return to Ft. Drum, I was told that my unit would ship off to Iraq in Feb. 2006. I knew that deployment was always a possibility but struggled with leaving my kids again; especially after having been separated them for so long during basic training and AIT. Ironically enough, I came up pregnant a couple of months after I got orders. I was relieved in a way but felt cheated in another. I knew that my "get out of jail free card" came in the form of me not being able to serve my country during a time that I was needed the most. A few weeks after my unit shipped out on February 28, 2006, I gave birth to my youngest daughter, Sharla. Although Henry and I's marriage became and remained rocky after he got caught cheating, my baby girl gave us a new sense of calm and peace that helped to camouflage the discord that had become embedded in the fiber of our marriage.

Once my four-year term was up, I traded in my love affair with Uncle Sam for stability. In order to preserve what was left of my marriage and maintain some semblance of a stable family life with Henry and the kids, I decided not to re-enlist. Since New Orleans was not a viable relocation option, Henry and I decided to move to Atlanta. Ms. Brazley, who was like family and one of the few people I stayed in touch with, lived there. She allowed us to stay with her until we were able to get on our feet. Henry landed a good job installing cubicles and other office furniture while I held it down at Dillard's department store until I landed a nice gig as a personal assistant.

Once again, Henry's devil horns started to show again once his volume of out-of-town jobs increased. Moving to Atlanta marked a new beginning in that I was excited to experience civilian life again but this time from a different perspective – I was married, had a *real* family, and was no longer flat broke. Henry and I also vowed to work on our relationship and to make a better life for our family. Trinity moved back from Mississippi to live with us, so it was the first time the four of us were under the same roof. In fact, Atlanta was full of "firsts" for us – we bought our first house, I went to an R. Kelly concert, which was the first one I had been to in years since first seeing him in Mississippi. It also marked the first time in our rocky marriage that my husband ever laid hands on me.

Around the same time that we moved to Atlanta, I discovered by accident that my ex, Trinity's father Gary, had also relocated to Atlanta from Mississippi. He had gotten far behind in his child support payments. Because the checks were sent directly to my daughter's caretakers at the time, I was unaware and had to pursue repayment through the Georgia court system. Pursuing this caused not only Gary to become bitter and angry towards me, but also sparked resentment in his live-in girlfriend, Lauran, who I ended up having words with on a few occasions.

It was on Memorial Day weekend of 2007. Henry and I had purchased our first home, which was one of the happiest days of my life. Unfortunately, once again Henry's devil horns started to show again. I found out later that he gave a friend of one of my friend's his phone number at our housewarming party and that was just the beginning.

That same summer, as Henry and I were settling into our home, the police showed up. Apparently Lauran had filed a false report claiming I harassed her. The police handcuffed me in front of kids that day and arrested me for harassment. But by God's grace and the truth, I never went to court on the charge and it was eventually dropped due to lack of evidence. Meanwhile, Gary was charged with Child Abandonment and ordered to pay the back-child support he owed.

Things only got worse from there. Hard to believe, but I was so naïve back then and believed everything Henry said. But something about me was different after I got out of the military. My love for music became my escape from the world around me and since Atlanta was a mecca for night life, good food and live music, I started to partake – sometimes with my husband and sometimes without.

Around the same time, my brother Alvin moved in with us, which helped in terms of support with the kids. Henry had become like Dr. Doolittle in the sense that he had taken up a weird interest in pets. I mean he had everything fish to rabbits to hamsters, which made for a full house. He also started to work out of town more and more around that time so was gone a lot, which gave him plenty of opportunity to cheat. I experienced everything from females who called our house all hours of the night, to discoveries of lip gloss and even a planted cell phone in his truck on one occasion.

He was good, an expert cheater, but like the habitual ones, he eventually would slip up and get caught. Each time he got caught, our arguments escalated to the point to where I would either throw him out or throw blows with him. It went from him pushing me out of his way, to him pushing me down, then punches to head, to a gun to the head while I was holding our youngest daughter Sharla. Even in those cases, I continued to make excuses for him. I told myself I was the reason I got hit and that the stress from his job caused him to lash out.

I don't recall exactly when or why, but I ended up going to Mississippi. This was the first time since the day I was ten and they took her away that I had seen Karen. She looked exactly the same way I remembered as a kid – dark-skinned, medium-build, with short, damaged hair. Not much had changed, but her mental illness was ever-present. Against my better judgement, I agreed to stay with her at her house. I felt like a fish out of water but gave it my best shot in an effort to reconnect and rebuild some semblance of a relationship with her. As part of her effort to rehabilitate and create a new life for herself after relocating from New Orleans, she had started back to college to earn her degree. I don't recall much of the visit except for the fact that it was awkward as hell; especially when she sent me to the store to buy my own dinner. She had fish in the freezer that I offered to cook for our dinner, but she declined despite my offer to reimburse her. That pretty much ruined the visit for me and any hope that we could somehow rebuild a relationship. I didn't see her again until 2014 at a relative's funeral.

Fast forward to 2008, R. Kelly went on trial for the remaining counts of child pornography and distribution and was found not guilty. That May he was performing in Atlanta, so I decided to go check him out. This was one of the first times and few times that I ventured out without Henry. It wasn't uncommon for members of Rob's entourage to survey the crowd for girls they thought he would like. And on this particular night, I was one of them. One of them spotted me in the crowd, came down, and got me. He took me backstage and there he was – the man himself, R. Kelly. He stood right in front me and flashed his pearly whites but seemed to look right through me as he made his rounds from table to table and stopped to socialize with the rounds of girls that his boys had pulled backstage that night. I guess I caught his attention enough to have one of his guys walk me out and make sure I got to my car safe.

"Yeah, you his type. He like 'em dark-skinned and petite," I remember his homeboy telling me.

"Really?" I was flattered.

"Yeah, he want you to follow the bus to the club so you can hang out some more."

"Ok," I said without hesitation. Yes, I was a married woman who was willing to follow a bus in hopes of sharing time and space with a man that I'd idolized for years. What was the harm in that? Afterall, he invited me to a public place, not a hotel room and as an adoring fan of the music not the man, I was not about to let the opportunity pass me by. But as fate would have it, I couldn't keep up with the bus and missed out on the opportunity. Instead, I went back home to an empty house and empty marriage.

About a year later, my suspicions of yet, another affair were confirmed when his mistress reached out to me on social media. Apparently during the time he was working in Alabama, he was also playing house and ended up getting his new girlfriend pregnant.

LISA: Ur profile pic on facebook…thx for the laugh and if I were u I wld invest in a spanxx…u actually do look like a celebrity…jamie foxx as wanda on in livin color…lol…First u were sayin I was a liar and tht Henry was not the father of my baby…tht I didn't knw who his dad was…I always knw who his dad was…ur husband…then u say tht im proud and that I gt wht I wanted….a baby from Henry….no…ths nt what I wanted…its always gonna b smthg with us….cause u always wanna b right…sorry doesn't wrk like that…even the best of us gotta b wrg sometimes…cnt always b wrg…the main tg u wnt is for us to g away so u cn live ur life happily ever after w Henry…lol. Once again it dnt wrk tht way either…

Just like Danesha, who managed to torment me during the first years of my marriage, Lisa kept her promise and made my life a living hell. After the initial shock of the affair and my husband's new baby wore off, I eventually forgave him. Call me naïve, desperate, or just plain crazy, but for some reason I believed everything he said. Despite being caught, he continued his affair with her, which caused things to quickly escalate. I endured months of her harassment by phone, email, social media and whatever avenue she could use, bragging about the details about not only where, but how she sexed my husband repeatedly.

She even managed to get Henry arrested for child-abandonment during a birthday party for one of the kids at Chuck-E-Cheese and eventually she had me arrested on false charges of harassment. The charges ended up being dismissed, but it was still a hard pill to swallow considering that this woman not only repeatedly slept with my husband but had the nerve to brag about it. She even continued to harass and threaten me at different points. She was relentless in her pursuit of Henry until my heart got tired and I finally tapped out.

CHAPTER 7 – CLOSE ENCOUNTERS

The next 2-3 years of my life were for the most part uneventful in the sense that Henry continued to cheat, his women continued to retaliate and stalk me, and I continued to turn the other cheek. In the meantime, I secretly kept in contact with a couple of members of Rob's entourage who kept me abreast of his appearances and other VIP opportunities. Although he continues to mischaracterize the situation in the media, Henry knew how much I loved R. Kelly back then for his music. I loved the music, not the man, but as our marriage started to deteriorate, Henry started to make snide comments about what he referred to as "my obsession" with R. Kelly. So it surprised me when he offered to take me to an all-white party where Rob was one of the headliners. It was the first time that we ever attended an R. Kelly concert together. It was also the last time…I filed for divorce shortly thereafter in 2013.

That May, Rob was back in Atlanta for Funk Fest, which was one of the biggest and baddest R&B concerts featuring Rob, Master P, TLC, and BBD. Damn-near all of my favorite artists at the time, all on one stage, all at the same time. Once again, I got all-access through his entourage but as much as I hoped that I would finally get to meet him, the opportunity didn't present itself that night either.

Fast forward to September when I had another close encounter with him in Atlanta. He had just started the promotions for his Black Panties tour and Atlanta was one of his first stops before hitting the road. I got invited to Club Reign, which was one of the hottest clubs in Atlanta at the time. One of the guys in his posse texted me earlier in the day to invite me to his first party but never sent back details. I don't know if I was pissed about the miscommunication or the fear of getting disappointed again by not getting to meet him, but at first I didn't want to go. Eventually my friend Tammy twisted both my arms. "It's your birthday weekend girl!" And just like that, my whole attitude changed.

When we arrived at the club, I immediately spotted one of the guys I knew, who invited me and Tammy back to the VIP area. No Rob. So when we were invited to go hang out at the afterparty, I agreed based on a hope and a prayer that I would still get to meet him; after all it was my birthday weekend. By the time we got to the after party, there were so many people there I barely got a glimpse of him, let alone the chance to meet him. Once again, I left disappointed.

Although we were clearly done, Henry refused to leave and made my life a living hell. Eventually the cussing matches turned physical. The last straw was when during one of our arguments, he slammed my finger in the door. I not only called the cops but slapped a stay away order on his ass so fast that he had no choice but to leave. He ended up moving in with his mistress-turned-wife and eventually filed for divorce at her insistence.

I got the call in January 2014 that, once again, Rob was in town and I was invited to hang out. This time I actually got the opportunity to sit down and talk with him face-to-face. As many times as I had been to Lenox Mall, never had the sights and stares been so vivid to me. Security was thick and so were we – I was one of 10-15 people; mostly dudes that surrounded him. As we walked through the courtyard in what seemed like slow motion, I mostly made small talk with the guys while he walked ahead of us and stopped at all the stores that were above my pay grade and even picked up a few things at some of them. Every once in a while, I caught a glance of him through the crowd but could never tell if he was looking back at me or at something else since he had on shades. He always had them damn shades on.

At one point he veered so close to me that I got a whiff of him and his freshness. He was always so fresh and well-groomed, which I loved. He mumbled something, but the loud chatter mixed with my anxiety about being in his presence, caused me to miss it. Instead of a response, I managed a fake laugh instead. *Shit, now he thinks I'm slow.* We walked a few more seconds in silence until one of his boys signaled for him to stop and take a picture with a fan.

After a few more laps around the mall, we eventually made our way to the main entrance of the mall. I spotted the convoy of black SUVs in the distance outside with black men in black suits and sunglasses, waiting for him like he was Barack Obama. I had enough sense to know I wasn't Michelle, so I stood back and waited for my cue. I noticed Rob stop and look back, but once again, I couldn't tell if I was the focus of his attention, so I looked away to play it off. He leaned in and whispered something in his homeboy's ear and then continued toward the exit in slow motion while his homeboy headed in my direction until he was in my face.

"Hey, Rob wants you to come back to the hotel with us. You down?"

"Yeah."

"Ok, where you parked?"

"On the other side by Cheesecake Factory."

"Ok, cool. Just come around and follow the black Escalade"

"Ok."

I nearly broke my neck as I made my way to my Honda, determined not to lose them this time around. I whipped around the corner just as the last Escalade pulled off.

I stayed a car distance behind them the entire way as we made our way through the streets of Buckhead until we got to the Intercontinental. I parked on the streets and waited a few minutes to allow time for Rob and his crew to make their way through the lobby doors. I noticed that three girls in hoe clothes near the entrance. They followed him in, so I figured they had been invited to the party too.

A few minutes later, I got out of my car and made my way in past the bellhops into the empty foyer. I wasn't sure which direction to go, so followed my military instinct and went to the right. In the distance, I saw Terrance wave his hand in a gesture that told me it was safe for me to follow him. I heard the familiar sounds of muffled chatter mixed with music in the background as we made our way down the hallway toward the suite. Once inside, it was a familiar scene – a bunch of dudes, more girls and Rob; only this time he wasn't surrounded by folks. He sat alone on a loveseat in the corner. He appeared to be on the phone, so I didn't approach. Instead I found an empty corner to stand in and waited patiently while Terrance grabbed me a drink.

As I waited, I periodically glanced over at Rob. At one point, our eyes connected long enough for him to gesture for me to come over to where he was. *Me?* I was nervous as hell but tried my best not to show it.

I wish I could tell you what we talked about that night, but I can't because I don't remember. Instead, I just remember that his lips seemed to move in slow motion and that he was funny, sexy, and charming all rolled up into one fine, tall, chocolate black man. For the next hour or so, we talked, and I laughed at each and every one of his jokes as we ate and sipped out of red Solo cups until one of his entourage signaled from down the hall. He tapped my leg and told me to hold on. A few seconds later, he re-emerged from around the corner and handed me a torn, yellow piece of paper with a phone number, that I assumed was his. He planted a soft and subtle kiss on my forehead and sent me on my way.

I contained my excitement long enough to get to my car. As cold as it was that night, I remember rolling down my window and inhaling in the cold Atlanta air. I rolled the window back up and grabbed my cell phone out of my purse.

ME: Hey, my name is Sante. I just made it to my car.

ROB: I know who you are.

I started my car, turned on *Bump and Grind*, which was my favorite R. Kelly song at the time, while I smiled and snapped my fingers all the way home.

CHAPTER 8 - DADDY

Dozens of text messages and a few weeks later on Valentine's Day weekend 2014, Rob and I consummated our relationship, so to speak. He had a concert in Baton Rouge the day before Valentine's Day that he personally invited me to. By this time, my contact with Terrance and other members of his entourage became non-existent since one of his rules was that we couldn't talk to anyone of the opposite sex, unless it was him. I learned later that there were many rules that came with being a part of Rob's world.

On this particular weekend, I was instructed to check into a room that had been reserved and pre-paid for and to be ready by 7 o'clock to head to the show that night. At 6:55 pm. I received a text to come to the lobby, which I did. Despite the baby weight I had gained over the years, I still managed to maintain my figure so that I was a stand-out anytime I attended one of his shows, because I never knew when I would be on display. That night was no different in the sense that I was given the opportunity to not only ride with him to the show, but once I we arrived, I received VIP treatment in the form of all-access to the finest accommodations and stage-side seating at what I considered to be the greatest show on earth.

After the concert, I waited for Rob backstage in his dressing room until it was time to ride back to the hotel. Although we barely said two words in the Escalade, the energy of our chemistry was in the air as we stepped into the empty elevator. As Rob took position behind me, his finger grazed my left thigh causing my body to instantly heat up. I inhaled through my nostrils and exhaled through the crack in my mouth, trying keep my composure, despite what I knew was about to go down.

Barry held the elevator door open as a white couple, a Hispanic-looking teenage boy and a middle-aged black woman got on and all migrated to the back where Rob stood. It was evident by the reaction on the Sista's face and her obvious glances, that she knew exactly who he was, whereas the others in the elevator had no earthly idea. Once Barry was in and the elevator doors closed, my nervousness re-emerged. *Oh shit, what do I do; should I press my floor or am I getting off with him on his floor?* I felt relieved when I peeped Barry out of the corner of my eye wave his keycard in front of the kiosk and press two floor buttons. One was my floor and the other I later discovered was Rob's.

What was only a few seconds, felt like forever. I stood there stiff as a board and stared straight ahead at the steel doors in front of me, trying to blend in. I pictured Rob as he stood behind me with his shades on and a half-chewed toothpick hanging from his lip, surveying my body from the heels of my black six-inch stilettos, which were killing my feet, to my ass cheeks which stood at full attention in my painted-on jeans. My mind suddenly shifted, and I wondered how many women he had been with that week or even the night before; knowing that I would soon be one of *them*.

I heard the **DING** of the elevator in the distance as I barreled down the hall, anxious to free my hooves from the heels, shower, and wait for Rob to text or call. I stood at the door and fumbled for my key card for a few seconds but was interrupted by the buzz of my phone. It was him.

ROB: Come to my room

ME: Ok

I forgot about my aching feet, my missing room key, and the shower I craved and instead made a beeline to the elevator where Barry was already there waiting. His extended arm to hold the elevator door open.

"Thank you," I said without making eye contact.

"You're welcome. 1147"

"What?"

"The room number."

"Oh ok," I replied, embarrassed at the thought of him thinking that I probably did this type of thing a lot.

It had to be pure adrenaline that carried me from the elevator, down the long hallway, and up to the door of the room at the end of the hall! I stood in front of room 1147, as I paused and gathered myself. I clutched my purse with one hand and lightly tapped on the door with the other.

In less than a second, the door opened and then closed behind me. My foot had barely touched the threshold before a set of unfamiliar, giant-sized hands gripped my ass. Without speaking a word, he leaned around and down to kiss me and then took my hand and led me into the darkness of the room that seemed to swallow me up. He gently released my hand, which allowed me to pause, look around, and examine the dimly lit room. I threw my purse on the sofa as he made his way to the bed. He had a white towel wrapped around his waist, so I figured that either he had just taken the fastest shower in history or was about to. Either way, I knew that six inches of heel separated me from the floor beneath. I sat on the couch and watched him as he stretched his long, slender body across the king-size bed and flat onto his stomach. I took off my shoes and allowed my toes to caress the carpet.

"Come here," he whispered almost as if someone else was in the room.

I walked toward the bed towards his outstretched hand.

"I need a massage. Come get on my back baby."

My nerves were back and pulsating, just like my heart, which was beating out of my chest by now. In my head I felt as if I wasn't fresh enough and wanted to take a shower bad – even a sink bath would've been fine at this point. Instead, I obliged his request, climbed onto the bed beside him, and positioned myself onto his lower back.

"Am I heavy?"

He laughed but didn't answer. The tightness of my jeans made the position uncomfortable, but in that moment I felt powerful, knowing that I was straddling the back of one of the sexiest, most desired, and legendary black men to ever walk the face of the earth. In my mind at the time, R. Kelly was every bit of the icon that Prince or Michael Jackson was – and then some.

"A little higher baby."

"Are my hands too rough? You got some oil or something?"

"Nahhhh, we don't need that. You good."

We made small talk for a few minutes about the tour, the weather, and how my massage was making his dick hard.

"You know I got a lot of girls right?"

"Yeah," I replied, not sure of what the right answer was.

"You cool with that?"

"Yeah."

"Good. Some of them are like wives to me."

"Really?"

"Yeah."

RECLAIMING MY POWER

I had so many questions but was too afraid to ask. As we continued to talk and laugh, he moved his arms from the folded position underneath his chin and reached back to stroke my thighs.

"You gotta come up outta these jeans girl. Come around here so I can help you."

He motioned his hands in a way that told me he wanted me front and center. He laid there for a minute looking up at me while I unsnapped, unzipped, and wiggled my way out of my jeans. He slowly made his way to his forearms and then to the edge of the bed with his legs open. He continued to stare. The imprint of his hard penis underneath the towel told me I was either in for a night of pleasure or pain. Either way, I didn't care. I wanted him *real* bad and by the way he stared and licked his lips, I knew he wanted me too.

I kicked my jeans to the side but left my thong in-tact. I pulled my top off over my head and then my bra. Without warning, he grabbed me by my ass, took both cheeks into his massive hands and pulled me toward him, in between his legs. He kissed my stomach gently then licked around and inside my belly button. It felt good to finally be touched again by somebody that I wanted to be touched by. I don't know if it was the power and prestige of Rob that turned me on, but I hadn't felt as excited or sexy in my entire twelve years of marriage to Henry. Or maybe it was the fact that I was never really attracted to my husband in the first place; or at least not like I was to Rob.

The thought of Henry who I imagined was back home either laid up with or about to lay up with another woman, left my head quicker than it entered. I grabbed Rob's bald head, which had beads of sweat on it and pulled it up and into my bare breasts. He cupped, kissed and nibbled on my nipples, taking them one by one in and out of his wet mouth. He then moved my thong to the side and inserted one, then two fingers inside of my wetness. I had never been the *fingering type*, but I went with it and allowed myself to enjoy it.

At a little over six feet tall and twice my weight, it wasn't hard for Rob to handle me the way that he did. He lifted me up like it was nothing, laid me on my back and pulled my wet thong off with one hand. He used his free hand to pull his towel off and threw it on the floor. He took my face into his hands and slid his tongue in and out of my mouth like he was making love to my throat. My insecurity crept in again as he went down on me like no one ever has since then and stayed down until I came. I had never been the *vocal-during-sex type* either, but I gave myself permission to be and so did he.

"Call me Daddy," he whispered. So I did. Over and over again.

CHAPTER 9 – FLY GIRL

I don't recall how long it took for us to finish what we started. I only remember that I was exhausted. I made my way towards the only light in the room. Carefully and slowly, I closed the door behind me and turned on the hot water before plopping down on the toilet to relieve myself. Once the water was hot, I took one of the hand towels on the shelf underneath the sink, soaked it and wrung it off. I wiped away the residue of sex mixed with regret, which was all over my body. I didn't regret the sex act itself at all, but I did regret the fact that I threw caution and common sense to the wind and had unprotected sex with a man I barely knew.

I took another towel and wrapped it around myself, opened the door and made my way over to Rob, who laid flat on his back and surprisingly was still fully erect. He was asleep so I tried not to wake him as I rubbed the warm towel up and down and around his penis. I dropped both towels on the floor and started to gather my clothes, which were scattered around the foot of the bed. No sooner than I had stepped into the first leg of my jeans, I heard his scruffy voice behind me.

"Hey, where you going?"

"To my room to shower."

"Not yet," he said and once again motioned his hand and patted the bed beside me where he wanted me.

We talked a few more minutes, had more sex and finally dozed off, but I barely slept because every time I moved, he moved. As soon as the sun showed itself through the window shades, I was outta' there. He was asleep and snoring, which made for an easy escape. I couldn't wait to get back to my room to shower. A few hours later, I received a text from him telling me to meet him in the lobby. It was close to checkout time, so I got my things together and made my way downstairs.

Barry greeted me at the elevator and pointed over to the corner area where Rob stood. As always, he looked like a million bucks sitting there with his shades, Gucci jogging suit, and J's to match, but my eyes went straight for the hand with the unmistakable Louis Vuitton symbol. He greeted me with a forehead kiss, which I thought was sweet at the time and handed me the bag which contained the Louis Vuitton bag that I had long sought after but could never afford. The only words that found their way to my lips were "Thank you." I didn't want to seem overanxious by saying too much, but I was. No one had ever given me a gift that was so nice and so expensive. Not even my own husband.

I told him I was headed to New Orleans, where I planned to celebrate my cousin's birthday and he told me that my room was taken care of and discretely handed me a wad of cash; $1,000 to be exact and told me to be safe and text him when I was headed back home to Atlanta. Twenty-four hours and several popped bottles later, I got back on the road back to Atlanta.

ME: Daddy, I'm heading back home.

He didn't respond, but I didn't take it personally but instead was content with our daily back and forth text communication. This occurred for the next several months along with several more invitations to concerts all around the country and occasional hook-ups at five-star luxury hotels. Sometimes I saw him after the show and sometimes I didn't.

In the meantime, my divorce from Henry became final on Jan. 26, 2015; which ironically was the same day 13 years earlier that we were married. Around that same time, I achieved another promotion in the form of "fly in" status, which meant that I was one of the girls that flew to whatever city Rob wanted me in. My kids, who were older by this time, usually stayed with Henry or with my neighbor, who I fully trusted. Shortly after being put into regular rotation, Rob also put me through a series of "tests" similar to what I later learned that the other girls had also gone through.

In March 2015, I flew to Chicago with the hope and intent on spending time with him. As always, he arranged luxury accommodations and threw in spending loot, as he often did. But it was always uncharted territory in the sense I that I never knew what to expect or if and when I would actually see him. On a typical trip, I usually spent my days in my pjs, watched TV, talked and texted to family and friends, and gorged on hotel snacks and room service until that call or text came through, which ultimately determined how I spent my day.

On this particular visit, it took two days before I heard from him. He texted me to come to studio, so I took a shower and called an Uber. Once I arrived at the studio, I texted him to let him know I was outside. He called right back, which surprised me and gave me butterflies at the same time. He asked me what I had on. When I told him he responded, "good girl." I was allowed to enter the studio but didn't get to see much of it since I was made to wait in a side room with a comfortable couch, a TV, and plenty of snacks. I didn't get to see him that day because he was "busy," but held out hope for the next day.

The next day I got a random text from Rob asking me how the weather was, which told me that he had been posted up at the studio the entire time without interruption. He told me to Uber to the studio and that his assistant would open the door to the Sprinter. I sat in the comfort and plushness of the Mercedes Benz Sprinter that day from around 11 am to 8 pm that day and passed the time by talking to friends and family on my cell.

ME: Daddy, I have to use the bathroom.

It felt awkward as hell as a grown-ass woman to ask for permission to use the bathroom but at that point in our relationship, I was willing to do whatever it took to please him. No response. At the point I felt my bladder ache, I searched my phone for restaurants in the area and found one in the vicinity. I relieved myself and headed back to the Sprinter where I made myself comfortable enough to fall asleep. Around 8 o'clock, one of the assistants came down and told me Rob was ready to see me. It was showtime.

I popped a peppermint, patted down my tracks, and applied a fresh coat of lip gloss. On one hand I was pissed, but on the other hand I was happy to be free from confinement and looked forward to seeing Rob. I've never been one to hide my facial expressions, but in this case I knew I had to. The inside of the studio was just like I imagined – darkness, reefer smoke, red Solo cups, and creativity energy filled the space. There was also a room full of unrecognizable faces, including women which I didn't expect. As Rob approached, I fake-smiled and leaned in to receive his kiss. We talked for about 5 minutes or less and then he was gone. I did my usual thing and settled into a corner and waited patiently for his return. And while he did return, in the meantime, it was like I was invisible as he worked the room and shot the shit with his boys. Around 4 am I had had enough. Rob was on one of the many couches in the room which were all full of dudes with a few females squeezed in-between them. I made my approach.

"Hey, can I talk to you."

"What up?"

"I gotta go. I got a red eye to catch in the morning."

"You serious?"

"Yeah."

I couldn't see past the shades but felt his blank, unconcerned stare. His response came out of nowhere.

"But I want you to stay." He turned the corners of his lips in the form of a frown.

I knew that staying another day would throw all of my plans into disarray, including the kids and my homegirl's schedule that agreed to keep them, but I stayed anyway.

"Ok, let me make a few calls."

"Cool."

The room was still crowded but I managed to find a quiet corner for some privacy to send a few texts. I noticed Rob get up and disappear into a room adjacent from where I stood. A tall, dark, older-looking chick followed him.

I took a seat in the spot where he sat, stared at the door, and waited. I wasn't mad or hurt or bothered by it all like most girls would've been. After all, he was straight up with me from the beginning when he first told me about his "other girls." Besides, I was too dead-dog tired to feel anything. Finally around 5 am, I called an Uber back to my hotel and slept like a champ. When I got up the next morning, I had a text from my homegirl who agreed to watch the kids for me another day, but no text from Rob.

ME: Hey Daddy, do you want me to come back to the studio?

Again, crickets.

A few hours after I didn't hear back, I found a flight back home. It was a very expensive flight, but I wasn't concerned because he always made sure I had a stash for situations like this and I always believed in saving for a rainy day – this was one of those rainy days.

I had been in Chicago for 4 days and spent a total of 5 minutes with Rob. A couple of days later when I did finally hear back from him, he didn't seem in the least bit phased that I was back home. We continued to text and FaceTime like it never happened.

CHAPTER 10 – TRAINING DAY

Fast forward to April 2016, Rob was on his Buffet tour and asked me to come to St. Louis for his show. Despite the occasional speedbump or two, I was enjoying the ride so I didn't mind his spur-of-the-moment requests. To me he was the perfect imaginary boyfriend. He made me laugh and smile more than all of the men I had ever been with combined and our sex was so electric that I didn't mind calling him Daddy. The expensive gifts and miscellaneous perks were all icing on the cake. We had very few conversations, but when we did talk it was always meaningful. We talked about everything from our kids, to his music and sometimes about his *other girls*. He always alluded to the other girls as his family, which made me nervous but still anxious to meet them. We had numerous conversations about their roles and his rules. He was grooming me for what came next and to expect the unexpected.

"My world comes with many rules ya know," he told me one day during one of our talks.

"Yeah, I know."

"I don't know if you can handle it."

What the fuck? I was confused and in disbelief. I've been with this man for almost two years. My ass has flown from city to city, sometimes at a moment's notice, and he has the nerve to question my strength and loyalty. I didn't bat an eye when I responded.

"I'm stronger than you think Rob."

So on the first day of the Buffet tour in St. Louis, my strength was put to the test. After the concert, we went back to the hotel but stayed on the bus which was parked in the back of the hotel parking lot. We usually rode back and forth to concerts in a Sprinter or black SUV, so I was excited to ride on the bus. It was plush as hell, almost like a house on wheels. The driver's seat was at the front, when you first entered, along with a privacy curtain that separated the front from the back, eliminating the possibility of seeing into the back of the bus.

Almost like an airplane, you had a thick curtain that separated the front section from the back. On each side, there were bench seats with small tables and a couple of bunk beds on either side of that. Then there was a bathroom followed by a short hallway which led to a nice-sized bedroom in the back. The bedroom was too small for a king bed but big enough for a queen bed and sofa chair.

Rob's assistant was the last one to leave the bus, leaving just Rob and I. When I put my phone up, it was around 3 am. We made our way back to the bedroom where we proceeded to drink and engage in everything from anal sex to fellatio and then some. Rob asked me to do things that night that we had not done up to that point and although I wasn't comfortable, I went with it and it all went so fast. I knew that this was the ultimate test, so I played the role of the submissive and did my best not to show my discomfort and in some cases my pain.

We fell asleep in-between licks and strokes, woke back up, and went at it again. We were going at it for damn near four hours. When I looked at the clock, it was close to 7 a.m. The sun had risen and made its way into the dark room through the cracks in the window curtains. I assumed he was sending for food when he leaned over and picked his phone up from the nightstand.

"Come here," he said in a groggy voice.

Within seconds, I heard a faint knock at the bedroom door. *What the hell,* I thought. I didn't hear the distinct sound of the bus door opening, so figured that who knocked was already inside of the bus.

"Come in."

When the door opened, a small-framed, light-skinned, butt-ass naked girl came in and closed the door behind her. She stood there for a minute, long enough for me to realize that she had been there the whole night and long enough for me to study her. She had a nice body – not a stretch mark on it from what I could tell in the darkness. Her breasts were full and round and big for her small frame but looked natural, so I surmised that they were hers. Her stomach was flat, which likely meant she didn't have any babies. When she turned around to shut the door behind her, I noticed that her ass was twice the size of mine but not as firm, which I admit made me feel a little better. Between her fixation with the ground and the braids that covered most of her face, I could barely see her face.. She slowly made her way over to the bed where we laid but we never made eye contact with one another. I started to get nervous at the thought of what I knew was about to go down.

"Bitch, get down on all fours!"

The words rolled off of his tongue so forcefully and commanding, almost like thunder. She instinctively fell to her knees and assumed the position.

Am I being punked?

"What's your name?" Rob asked her.

"Juice," she said in a voice that resembled a cartoon character.

"How old are you?"

"Thirty-one?"

"How long have you known me?"

"Sixteen years Daddy"

I did the math in my head and figured that they had been around each other since she was 15.

"Good girl, now get up."

He motioned for her to come closer and sit down as he made his way, erection and all to the other side of the room and sat on a narrow bench. I figured Juice wasn't a mind-reader but that she had played this scene so many times before that it was second nature to her. She knew exactly what she was supposed to do. She picked up the iPad that was on the table that separated us and started the music.

"Come and suck Daddy's dick."

I watched as Juice went to him, got down on her knees and started sucking and slurping on him like he was her breakfast, lunch, and dinner.

He tilted his head back in pleasure and then looked at me, grabbed her braids and guided her head to move faster up and down his shaft. He backed her off by pulling her back by her braids, long enough to catch his breath and composure.

"She's my trainer and she is going to teach you how to please Daddy like that, ok?"

He motioned for me to come over to where he stood while Juice continued to suck, slobber and twist on his dick with her tiny hands. I was still dazed and confused but did as he instructed.

"Ok."

"Get up and kiss her," he instructed Juice. And so she did. I felt her tongue against my lips but didn't open my mouth to kiss her back.

"Now eat her ass out like Daddy eats you."

As she made her way back down towards the floor, she gently spread my legs and started to lick from the top of my landing strip down to my labia. Rob then instructed me to suck his dick, which I managed to do, as uncomfortable as I was in the presence of Juice. This was far from what I imagined my first ménage à trois to be like.

He hadn't yet climaxed at that point, nor had I, so he tapped Juice to get up. He then took my hand and laid me on the bed. Juice came in behind us as if she already knew what to do. For the next few minutes, the three of us exchanged kisses, juices and moans before Rob got up and made his way back to the chair. On his way, he grabbed the iPad and I assumed by the way he held it up that he was recording us. Although I was nervous, but I didn't say a word. Instead Juice and I continued to follow his instructions.

"Oh this is good," he belted out at one point. I glanced over and watched as he jacked-off with one hand and held the iPad with the other. When he reached over to pull back the blind behind him, I panicked.

"Yeahhhhh, I want everybody to see this."

Thankfully the bus windows were frosted so nobody could see in.

After he climaxed and washed himself off in the sink, he told Juice to leave.

I thanked God it was over. I wanted to scrub myself down and wash all evidence of my first threesome away, but didn't get a chance to. Rob came over, got on top of me and we started to have sex again. When we finished, he made his way to the front of the bus where Juice was. I followed him and put my clothes back on. He remained naked and so did she. None of us said a word; most likely because we were all exhausted from over an hour of sexcapades. Juice finally broke the silence.

"Daddy, I'm hungry, can I go eat?"

"Go ahead."

I wanted to go with her but couldn't get past the fact that she had to even ask in the first place. After Juice put on her clothes and left, Rob and I made our way back to the bedroom where we continued to have sex.

About an hour later, we both showered, got dressed and prepared to head to the next city, which was Kansas City. Once again, I hung out onstage, sang all the words, and got back on the bus. This time it didn't bother me because of what I experienced earlier in the day. I needed the space to recuperate and process everything that had happened. I went back to my hotel and flew back to Atlanta the next day without saying goodbye.

ME: *Hey Daddy, I made it home.*

ROB: *Ok baby, see you soon.*

ME: *When?*

ROB: *Soon enough*

I made it a point in the weeks that followed to get myself checked out. The instances of unprotected sex with not just Rob but now his other girls, did not sit well with me. As much as I tried to inspect myself and him whenever the opportunity presented itself, I refused to let my ignorance get me a life sentence in the form of an incurable disease. Thankfully all of my tests, even my recent ones, have all come back clean.

RECLAIMING MY POWER

CHAPTER 11 – MÉNAGE À TWICE

My "soon enough" came a couple of months later in June when Rob flew me to Houston for a show. I stayed posted up at the St. Regis until he finished. When he got back to the hotel, he texted me to come to his room.

It was around 2:30 a.m. when I knocked at his room door. To my surprise, instead of Rob, I was met by a chick about my complexion, maybe a little bit darker. She was slim like me, but a little thicker. It was dark so I couldn't see her face, but over time all of *Rob's girls* became faceless to me. She had shoulder-length, wavy, weaved hair. I was certain I had never seen her before. We exchanged fake smiles and quickly sized each other up as I walked in. Rob sat on a sofa in the corner of the living area, which was dimly lit from the TV on the other side of the suite.

He summoned both of us to come to him and gave me dick duty while he fingered the other girl, who was already undressed. The room smelled of weed, Hennessy, and fish. I couldn't tell if they had been eating seafood or if the smell was from the mystery chick, which gave me concern. Once again, I knew what was about to go down.

Eventually we moved into the bedroom where he instructed me to undress and lay down while the other girl stood. I could tell she had done this many times before and knew exactly what to do. She had obviously been trained by Juice. As I lay there, my stomach started to knot up. I saw Rob grab a black velveteen bag from the top drawer. At first I thought he was about to record the scene, but instead he pulled out a pretty thick navy-blue dildo from the bag. *Oh shit. It's about to get freaky up in here* was my first thought, since this was the first time he had ever introduced a toy into the mix.

He laid down next to me while the chick reassumed her previous position and continued to give him head. I expected him to insert the dildo into me but instead he stuck it into himself! As I lay there watching in discomfort and disbelief, thinking to myself, *What the fuck?!* I couldn't believe what I witnessed. I guess he could feel my tenseness, because he whispered, "It's ok baby. Just lay on Daddy's chest." His breath deepened and his hand-stroke did too. I continued to lay there and held my breath, unsure of what to do with my hands or my mouth. Once again, the thought entered my head, *"Am I being punked?"*

After he came, the girl went into the bathroom to get a towel to clean him off. I was thankful it was over and that I didn't have to mix spirits with a stranger again. But I was wrong. We marched single file back into the living room, where we continued with our sexcapades. I had learned to fake my orgasms like a pro so when he was satisfied with the notion that we were both satisfied, he joined us on the sofa and we eventually dozed off. A couple hours later I woke up in a mangled mess of arms and legs and was hungry, so Rob ordered room service. We didn't say much, but instead watched TV and ignored the elephant in the room.

Finally, one of Rob's assistants knocked on the door and told us to head downstairs to the Sprinter. I knew I still needed to go back to my room to pack and shower, so I asked for more time. She gave me ten minutes, but being the rule-breaker that I was, I took twenty. That was a big mistake! By the time I got dressed, gathered my things, and made it outside, the Sprinter was gone. No assistant, no security, no chick, and no Rob. Obviously panicked, I called Rob but got no answer. I texted him a couple of times and still got no response, so I called but a bad connection quickly disconnected us. As a last resort, I texted a number he had given me but told me to never call – another one of his rules. When that didn't work, I called the number, but my calls went straight to voicemail. It was then that I realized the number belonged to Juice.

With all options exhausted, I took an Uber to the closest rental car facility I could find and as much as I hated to, I made the 4-hour trip to Dallas. Why? One part of me was afraid of Rob's wrath and the potential for him to cut me off, whether this was one of his many tests or if he thought I ghosted him in some way. The other part of me felt guilty and thought it was my fault that I didn't follow instructions and took longer than I was told when I knew the crew had a schedule to keep.

Thankfully, my friend Tonya lived there so I knew that if I didn't catch up with Rob and crew, I had a place to chill until I was able to make my way back to Atlanta. When I made it to Dallas, Tonya was waiting for me at the rental car location. We had just enough time to change clothes at her house before we headed to the venue where Rob was to perform. On about the umpteenth try, I finally reached him.

"Hey Daddy, I been trying to call you. I'm here at the concert?"

"What do you mean? You on the Sprinter right?"

"No, you guys left me."

"What do you mean, you got left? How did you get to Dallas?"

I ignored his first question. He was obviously pissed.

"I rented a car. Ummmm, but I tried to call you and texted Juice, but she ignored my texts."

"We almost at the stadium so just stay put and I'll holla when we comin' through, ok? And you just need to fall in behind us."

As expected, we got stopped by security as we tried to fall in behind the Sprinter and Rob's tour bus. Eventually we got in and one of the assistants came to get me. I was allowed to go backstage to Rob's room, but Tonya was given an all-access wristband and escorted to the front of stage. I was excited to see him but somewhat nervous because of the scenario. I was also pissed at the thought that Juice had purposely ignored my text. As time went on, I became hip to the game. If we were paid prostitutes, Juice would be considered the "bottom bitch" in that she had been in Rob's stable for the longest. Because of this, she got special treatment and he let her slide on a lot of things, including broken rules that he would've nailed me to the cross for.

His distinctive scent entered the room before he did. As always he was dressed to impress, complete with gold chains and shades.

"You supposed to stand up when the king comes through." He peered down over his shades and looked dead at me. I laughed nervously but when I saw that he didn't return the laugh, I sprung up like a shudder.

"Hey Daddy." I walked over and leaned in to kiss him.

He accepted the kiss and clasped my waist with both hands and pulled me in close enough to whisper in my ear.

"When a king walks in the room, you supposed to stand up. I don't care if I walk in and outta' this muthafucka' ten times, you still stand up. Ok?"

"Ok Daddy."

As always, Rob put on a great show that night. We all watched in amazement from just offstage, sang all of his songs, and danced like we had all the money in the world but not a care to match it. After it was all over, we were escorted backstage. I was excited more so for Tonya since she had never met him before, but instead of acknowledging me or her, the first question out of his mouth was directed at Juice.

"Did you enjoy the show baby?"

RECLAIMING MY POWER

"Yes Daddy."

"How did she do?"

"She danced and knew all of the words."

"Cool," he said.

As relieved as I was that I had gotten the gold star and met with Rob's approval, I couldn't help but be pissed at the fact that I was being watched like a middle schooler and that he acted so cold earlier. In that instant he was a far cry from the funny, charismatic Rob I had come to know and fall in love with.

Juice, his assistant, and I waited in his dressing room while Tonya was escorted to another waiting area. Cathy and Rob made their way to one of the rooms located on the far end of the dressing room. I said very little but felt a lot. If I had to describe the feeling, it was like confusion with a mixture of "pissed off" at the fact that I had been instantly bumped down to the bottom of the food chain. As we sat there in silence, we all did our best to ignore the moans and other sex sounds coming out of the backroom. Instead, we fiddled with our phones and made small talk. When the moans got too loud, Juice went back and knocked on the door to signal that they were too loud. They eventually lowered the volume but by that time I guess it was time to go. The assistant instructed me to head to the Sprinter while Juice went to the bus.

I had my homegirl follow the caravan to the next stop, which was a strip club. Next stop was an after-hours club and finally, as the sun made its debut, we ended up back at the W Hotel where Tonya and I exchanged kisses, hugs, and plans to hook up the next day. I guess Rob's assistant overheard us, because she immediately told me to get my bags before I ended up in the next city without clothes.

The next city? As much as I wanted to know where we were headed, I didn't ask questions. Afterall, I felt like a free agent during the summer months since the kids were with Henry. I knew they were clean and safe, so I thought of this as my time. I was a grown, single woman with cash in hand, traveling from city to city having consensual sex with a man that I thought I was in love with and that would eventually choose me. So I grabbed my bags out of my homegirl's trunk and made my way into the lobby to get my room assignment. Rob and I had barely said two words to each other that night, so I was surprised he even wanted me to travel to the next city, which was Oklahoma City, I found out later. We arrived at the OKC venue the next day just in time for Rob to go onstage and as usual, me, Juice and Cathy were escorted to our designated area alongside the stage to put on our usual dog and pony show. We sang every word, danced and secretly competed to get his attention from the stage. After the show we went back to the hotel and were told to wait in our rooms until someone came to get us. That was another one of Rob's rules, to always wait until someone came to get us and to never wander off without permission.

Just like Dallas, I got no texts, phone calls or knocks at the door that night, so instead I used the time to talk to the kids and get a good night's sleep. The next morning around checkout time, I got the text to report to the Sprinter downstairs. Rob was already on the bus with Juice and Cathy and I ended up in Sprinter with two of his female assistants. I had become used to traveling with Evelyn and Roz. For some reason, Rob always wanted his girls separated and since I didn't too much care for Juice anyway, I didn't mind. Besides, it gave me a chance to talk freely since Rob preferred little to no conversation amongst any of his staff. He preferred for us to be silent and invisible. We were not to be seen or heard most of the time. If we traveled alone, he told us to wear earphones so that we whoever we were with would be less likely to engage in conversation with us. He was always paranoid about his personal business being discussed. He frequently asked if I was following this rule and I always confirmed, although sometimes I lied.

On this particular trip, I remember the dialogue being extra lax. We sat there for what felt like days and made small talk about Rob's favorite gumbo recipe and even talked shit and took pot shots at Cathy and Juice. Neither of them mentioned the city we were headed to and I didn't ask. By the time we finally stopped, I was relieved and ready to get off, stretch my legs and settle into whatever luxury hotel was chosen for us that night. A few minutes after we stopped, one of Rob's male assistants knocked at the door and said that Rob wanted to see me.

Finally, I get some time. That was my first thought. My second thought was to pop a peppermint, spray some smell good, and fix myself up.

I got out of the Sprinter and took a seat on one of the narrow stairs and waited for Rob to make his way from his bus to where I was perched. I stood up when I saw him and as I made my way to him, caught a glimpse of his distinctive smile. It made me smile and heat up at the same time.

"Where's your phone?" He asked abruptly.

"In there Daddy." I pointed behind me in the direction of the Sprinter.

"Go get it."

I immediately tensed up at the thought that I was somehow in trouble. Occasionally I was told that Rob would ask to check the girls' phones to make sure we weren't communicating his business or with other dudes. This was a first for me, but I was prepared. As I trotted to the Sprinter, I caught a glimpse of him in the side mirror watching me.

When I returned with my phone I peeped Cathy and Juice's exit from the bus. They were headed in our direction. I handed him my phone but to my surprise he handed it right back to me. He turned in the direction of Juice and Cathy and made an unfamiliar gesture to them. They immediately sped up their stroll toward me and almost like robots, stopped and leaned in to hug me.

The four of us walked toward what appeared from a distance to be a party in the park. As we approached, we learned it was a festival and a strategic stop in our trek to God knows where. There were live bands, lots of families, rides, and food trucks. We walked around for a while but were eventually forced to leave when people started to notice Rob. As much as Rob loved his fans, he was always very private and particular when it came to signing autographs and taking pictures.

It was at the next stop that I finally realized our location, but still had no idea on destination. We stopped to eat at a Red Lobster in Mississippi. Almost immediately after I returned to the Sprinter with the assistants, my stomach started to bubble. I didn't know if it was from the food or something else, but I had a serious case of the bubble guts. I tried to sleep it off but when that didn't work, I asked permission to use the bathroom at the next stop but was told to wait.

Being the rebel and grown-ass woman that I was and always will be, that didn't sit right with me, so I jumped off after one of the assistants got off to grab something from the store. I had no idea if I would be left or worse, get a lashing when I got back and didn't give a damn either. Rob had never laid hands on me, but I didn't put it past any man. My tough-as-nails interior and exterior was ready for whatever the punishment was. Lucky for me, the caravan was still there and instead my punishment for disobedience came in the form of Juice and Cathy who were both posted up in the Sprinter when I got back. Again, I didn't ask questions, but instead tried to sleep off the rest of my bubble guts in hopes that we would reach our destination – wherever that was – very soon.

RECLAIMING MY POWER

CHAPTER 12 – END OF DAYS

Week 1

I was awakened by the tremble of the Sprinter as it steadily slowed to a slow creep and eventually to a complete stop. The familiar sound of air releasing from brakes, coupled with the squeak of the double doors as they slowly opened, was music to my ears. Finally, a chance to relieve myself, shower, and hopefully get some much-needed sleep.

"Welcome home babies!" Rob's voice appeared out of nowhere and commanded our attention. The five of us sprung up in the presence of "the king" and made our way down the short set of stairs in single file. I had seen pictures of the house before, so knew that we were back home in *Hotlanta*; the John's Creek subdivision of Atlanta, to be exact. This was Rob's second home away from home. The apartment in Chicago's Trump Tower was his primary residence, in addition to the studio he owned there.

In true Pied Piper fashion, he led us in with his all-too-familiar whistling sound and wave of his hand and gave us a tour of his 11 thousand square-foot compound. My stomach was about to explode but I managed to hold it in by contracting every muscle in my body. The foyer area was already lit as if whoever was there expected us. I found out later that there were two other girls who stayed there from time to time and were allowed to come and go as they pleased since they were in school.

Two king-size chairs adorned the hallway along with a white grand piano just off to the side in what resembled a dining area, just in front of the iron-wrought staircase. Just to the left, behind the French doors sat a nice-sized sofa, three chairs and a small bar area. We made our way to one of Rob's three living areas, which were all pretty nicely sized. One of the living spaces led directly to his bedroom, which was the only bedroom downstairs in the eight-bedroom house, while the other living areas were closer to the kitchen.

Cathy and I followed him upstairs while Juice and the assistants made themselves comfortable in the main living area. I assumed that Juice was already familiar with the layout and that she more than likely had a room upstairs that she had laid claim to long before us. As we made our way through the maze-like hallway upstairs, I noticed a pattern to the bedrooms – each had its own distinct color or color scheme. There was a pink room, a blue room and the room I came to dread the most, the Black Room. Given his superstar status as a pioneer in the industry, I expected *THE R. Kelly* to have a much grander home but as I later discovered, along with the rest of the world, everything that glittered with Rob definitely wasn't gold. The house was later foreclosed on in 2018, around the same time the rest of his shit started to hit the fan.

I didn't ask for permission when I made my exit and beeline to the bathroom to handle my business. When I was finished, I rejoined Cathy and Juice upstairs to get situated and settled into our rooms. As suspected, Juice had her own room, which was one of the larger rooms at the other end of the hallway. My room was a Hawaiian-themed room with a nice-sized bed and a chair in the corner. There was also a pool table, which seemed misplaced to me, along with a TV and two dressers. My room, along with a couple of others, overlooked the pool. It was a nice room and a nice house in general, but I knew I wouldn't be there long, despite Rob's insinuation about making it our new home. Afterall, I had a life on the other side of town, complete with kids, plans, and expectations. I gave myself until July when I knew my son would celebrate his birthday, which was around the corner from the start of school.

As much as I hate to admit, it felt good at the time to have passed another one of Rob's ultimate tests and the reward was him moving me in. It took me getting past the point of wanting to please him, at any cost, before I realized that it was all a part of his manipulation game and master plan. Whether it was a couple of months or in my case, a couple of years; he would assess his girls to see where they stood mentally and emotionally to see if he could control their minds enough to bring them to the point of total dependence on him. Once he had you, he moved you in. It didn't matter if you were 16 or 36, like I was at the time; his goal was to gain complete and total control over your mind, your body, and your freedom.

It had been over 24 hours since my last shower, so I couldn't wait to wash my ass, unpack, and eat. Rob told us to meet him downstairs in the cigar room once we got settled, where we listened to music and made small talk for a while before he dismissed us and told us to get some rest. He instructed Juice and I to meet him in the Black Room later, so I set my alarm before I laid it down. I was hungry but since no one offered up any food, and I didn't dare ask. Instead I snacked on the chips and soda I had tucked away before I drifted off to sleep.

A couple of hours later, I was awakened to the sound of *Love Letter*, which was one of my favorite songs at the time and my ringtone. I brushed my teeth, freshened up, and took a deep breath before exiting my room and proceeding to the Black Room down the hall. I never knew what to expect with Rob.

The door was cracked, so I tapped it lightly before I entered. One of the rules was that you always knocked before you entered. Since no one responded, I assumed that I was the first to arrive, so I entered. There was a small lamp in the corner by the bed, which allowed me to get a semi-clear view of the dark room. Everything was black and I do mean *everything*, from the walls to the curtains to the bedding, sofa, and chairs. Even the shag rug was black. I peeked into the adjoining bathroom and noticed that it was also blacked out from the sink, to the toilet, even the bathtub/shower. I had never seen anything like it.

About an hour passed and no one came. Since there was no TV, I laid across the bed and stared at the ceiling, which was also black. Rob's entry into the room startled me at first, but I stood up, assumed the position and greeted him with a kiss. My heart sank a little when Juice entered right behind him. She and Rob took positions in the chairs across from one another almost as if they were rehearsing for one of his performances. I nervously took a spot on the loveseat between them. What happened next set the tone for my next three weeks in the house.

For the next few hours, the three of us engaged in the most vile and demeaning sex imaginable. As many times I thought about saying NO or getting my shit and leaving, something inside wouldn't let me. Oddly enough, I still wanted to please Rob and despite the fact that I hated the acts themselves, what I hated even more was the fact that they were almost always videotaped and always without our consent. Most of the time, he watched and directed while Juice or one of the other girls watched. Other times, he engaged while Juice directed.

When he was finished, he dismissed us – Juice went in one direction while I went in another and Rob nonchalantly trotted downstairs to his master suite.

The next couple of days, for the most part, were uneventful. There were no calls for breakfast or lunch or anything, for that matter. Instead, I stayed in my room and occupied my time on my cell phone since my repeated requests and pleas to connect the cable in my room were ignored. In the weeks I called Rob's house *home*, we left our rooms only when we were summoned, we ate when Rob ate, and if Rob didn't like what we wore, we changed our clothes. When we ventured out, it was rarely alone and only to the studio or the mall. When we were in his presence, we had to ask to use the bathroom, bathe, and/or shower as well. I remember being at the point of lightheadedness on either day 2 or 3 when I texted Rob to ask if I could eat. To my surprise, he texted right back and told me to come downstairs to get the keys to the Tahoe. I ran around the corner to get chicken, biscuits and sides for me, Rob, and the girls and made a pitstop at the gas station where I picked up snacks like dry cereal, chips, and powdered donuts for my private stash. These things came in handy on days when I wasn't offered so much as a peanut, let alone a meal.

Rob had a couple of shows in the Carolinas, so we all hit the road again after a few days in the house, which was a much-needed break for me. The isolation, the rules, and the constant sex had gotten to me and were a catalyst for my anxiety, depression, and extreme longing for home and my family. Every day it seemed like a new rule was imposed. Not only were we required to knock and wait for a response before we entered a room, but if we were upstairs and wanted to come downstairs, we were told to stomp on the hardwood floors until we were told to come down. One day, I remember going downstairs without stomping and entered one of the main living areas without announcing myself. Rob was posted up in the corner with another young chick that I had only seen in passing. She was on her knees giving him head.

"Oh shit, I'm sorry."

Fire was in his eyes and in his response.

"Now what if I was fucking a rabbit?! Then I would have had to kill you."

I opened my mouth to respond but not a word came out. I didn't know if he was serious or not, so I scurried my ass back upstairs, shut my door and waited for my punishment, which turned out to be more filthy sex in the Black Room later that day.

Week 2

After a week I was almost out of clothes so asked Rob if I could make the trip across town to get more.

"Damn, we are about to leave to go to the studio. Can you be back by 4:30?"

By this time it was about 3:45 so I knew, and he did too, that there was no way in hell I could make it across town and back in Atlanta traffic.

"No Daddy, not in traffic."

"So just go when I'm asleep."

I thought, *Hell, you barely sleep,* but didn't dare let the words escape my mind or my mouth.

He added, "when you go home, bring everything, because you will be living here with Daddy."

I did my best to keep a straight face but knew there was no way on God's green earth that would ever happen.

"Daddy, you don't like feeding people and I love to eat."

"What the fuck did you just say?"

My humorous rebound was obviously an epic fail. He told me "don't ever say that shit again," then asked me what I wanted to eat and headed out to the studio. I was outdone so retreated to my room. I didn't see him or anyone again that night.

The next morning, I woke up not only hungry but without a fresh change of clothes…again.

ME: Daddy, can I get an Uber to go home and get some clothes?

ROB: Cum to the Black Room.

I was pissed because I knew I would go another day without my clothes from home and because sex was the last thing on my mind at the time. For the umpteenth time since I had been there, I met Juice and Rob in the Black Room for threesome action. Before we got to it, he told Juice to go check on "her sister," referring to Cathy to make sure she was asleep, which I found odd. But then again, everything about Rob, who turned into R. Kelly before my eyes, was odd to me.

When she returned, she confirmed that Cathy was asleep so we both stripped down instinctively. As usual, he pulled his pants down and put me on dick duty first, while Juice took position behind him. I was able to look up between blows and strokes where I spied their passionate exchange of slobs and tongue kisses. I also noticed that Juice's finger(s) was inserted in Rob's ass. Her wrist made a jab and poke movement which seemed to give him a hell of a lot more pleasure than I was giving him.

Eventually he stopped and made his way to the dresser where he pulled out his black bag of tricks. *Oh no, not this shit again.* Anxiety and discomfort gripped my body. This time the dildo was double ended; one side was long, thick, and straight while the other side was short and curved in the shape of a hook. I didn't know what to think. *Did Rob secretly prefer dick and I just didn't know it?* Afterall, the pleasure he got from self-penetration seemed to far surpass the pleasure he got from sex with any of us.

Something had changed; not necessarily with Rob, but maybe with me? I was no longer comfortable, and the shit wasn't fun or electric anymore. Furthermore, Rob was definitely not who I thought he was. He was the R. Kelly that I had always denied existed. At any rate, when he finished, he once again told Juice to make sure Cathy was still asleep and once again she returned to the room to confirm that she was.

A day or two later, I witnessed one of the most disgusting and degrading scenes I'd ever seen, which was one of the final straws for me. A few of us girls were in one of the living rooms where we were watching the ID (Investigation Discovery) channel, which ironically was Rob's favorite channel. A girl named Sarah who I hadn't seen around very often but looked barely to be out of high school was there that day. From what one of the assistants told me, she had just graduated high school and was entering her freshman year of college.

Out of the blue Rob told her to come to where he sat on one of the sofas and get on all fours. I had never seen him expose himself in front of any of his assistants, but that day he did. He pulled his penis out of his pants so casually, almost like he was pulling out his wallet and without instruction, Sarah started to suck it. She sucked it like she owned it and with enjoyment, right there in front of me, Cathy, Juice and Rob's assistant. It made me sick to my stomach, especially when I thought about the fact that my oldest daughter was around her age. I turned my head, while the others watched and once he exploded in her face, we all returned to our regularly scheduled programming as if nothing had ever happened. That day will forever be etched in my memory as the day that I lost respect for Rob. That was also the day that he transformed, in my mind, to the monster that everyone said he was.

Week 3

With plenty of time, silence, and opportunity on my hands, I started to work on my exit strategy from the house. Rob spent more and more time at the studio in preparation for an upcoming show in New Orleans, so I made my plan to leave the Sunday morning after the show. I still had people in the city that I knew I could depend on to pick me up and protect me if some shit popped off. Besides, I had plenty of cash, which I had saved up while the other girls spent theirs at the mall.

My Plan B became Plan A on the Monday before that concert when Rob scolded me like a two-year in front of the other girls and his entourage for wearing a tank top. Apparently, the other girls were "intimidated by my choice of clothes," so I was instructed to change and to cover up like the other girls. The other girls mostly wore track suits and jogging sets, even in the dead of May. Instead of entertaining another argument, I took my tongue-lashing like a woman, covered up with a jacket and kept my mouth shut.

RECLAIMING MY POWER

A couple of days after that on the Wednesday before we were to leave for New Orleans, my tolerance was once again tested when Juice and I got into it. I don't recall what exactly set it off but I remember that she got pissed when I ignored her request to help her get some bags from the car. It quickly escalated and damn-near got physical when she sent Cathy to ask and I ignored her too.

"You got a problem with me?"

She got in my face so close that I smelled her breath.

"I sure do!"

Before I knew it, one of the assistants jumped in between us. Rob came running out of the house with cell phone in hand. He grabbed my arm, pulled me to the side and proceeded to question me like I was the guilty one. As much as I tried to plead my case, his mind was already made up and he was clearly on Juice's side. He accused me of having "black woman's syndrome" because "you got a mutha-fuckin' problem anytime another black woman tells you what to do," he said, "especially a younger black woman!" That was the final straw.

We argued for another few minutes or so until we both went mute and I asked to go to my room. As soon as I got there, I shut the door behind me and called my homegirl Rhonda to come pick me up. I was completely done. She didn't work far from where I lived, so I knew she could come quickly, before I had a chance to change my mind and before Rob or anyone else could talk me out of my decision to leave. It didn't take me long to pack my shit. When Rhonda pulled up, Rob and a couple of guys from his crew were still outside standing around.

I didn't give her a chance to call or honk; I marched straight to the trunk without making eye contact with Rob or anybody else in his crew. My eye was on the prize – my freedom – and nothing else mattered.

"Is that your Uber?"

"Yes."

And just like that it was over – those were our final, parting words to one another.

A week later, he called and asked if I was ready to apologize. I had mixed emotions because on one hand, I was relieved to hear from him and that he thought enough of me and what we had, to reach out. On the other hand, I was angry that he let me go in the first place. I had to dig deep, but once I did, the old Asante came back and I managed to stand my ground. I had finally reclaimed my power. I told him in no uncertain terms that I didn't have shit to apologize for. He ended the call with an offer to come home and the promise that he would send for me when I was ready to apologize.

"You got a week to do it and if you don't, lose my number."

I never made that call and took him up on his offer to lose his number. I never called, texted, or saw him (in person) again...

CHAPTER 13 – WHEELS DOWN

"How can people be so cruel. You have all this evidence and see all of this stuff dated back to the '90s and you want to attack me"…I shut down. I didn't want to leave my house. I wanted to sleep everything away and hoped it would have a different outcome. But it wouldn't stop, it still hasn't stopped!

As the words flowed out of my mouth, my emotions took over me all over again. It was my first real trigger since my visit to the house that I called home for three weeks, nearly a year ago when Lifetime first aired the first part of its docuseries *Surviving R. Kelly*.

"Can we take a break?" I caught a glimpse of the camera man as he gave a signal to CUT. My hands trembled as I brushed my bangs away from my eyelashes which I felt loosening their grip from the wet corners of my eyes. The look I got from the female producer was one of *Bitch, this is your third break,* which translated to NO.

I didn't want to be there in the first place, especially after all of the empty promises they made and never intended to fulfill, in my opinion. And although I had mixed emotions when I first got the call to come back for Part II of the docuseries, all of the old emotional demons found their way back into my spirit, but were more extreme this time around. Feelings of anger and resentment took over after I, along with the other "R. Kelly survivors," repeatedly asked for help that never came. We asked for counseling as a form of escape from the sunken place we had all fallen into when we decided to speak up and speak out against R. Kelly. Instead, my emails went unanswered and my phone calls went unreturned. And when the network did finally reach out, they told us that in-person therapy *wasn't in the budget* even though we all knew full and well that they profited from our pain. I've always felt that I took the biggest hit reputationally with all of the shit they drug up from my past.

I cleared my throat and gave my nod of approval to continue.

"They even pulled out my mugshots," I looked directly into the camera and tried hard to contain myself. "Yes, I was arrested. I was not convicted…they are waiting to get that news that survivor Asante McGee is dead from suicide..."

I felt my voice crack but allowed my tears to flow this time.

An hour later, it was done. It was finished. I politely exchanged half hugs and handshakes and set my intention to never step foot in this studio again. I inconspicuously made my exit out of one of the doors that led to the loading dock. The warmth of the California sunlight felt nice on my face but Malcolm's smile as he stood in the distance with his hand extended outward, waiting to clasp mine, was even nicer. He wore the same white starched button-down, Gucci belt, and Gucci loafers as when he first picked me up days ago, which was a sign of not only of a full circle moment but also evidence of closure.

"You good Ms. McGee?"

"Yessssss. Just ready to get home."

"Well, you're on your way. I'll have you there in a few."

Just over an hour and a kiss on the cheek later, I settled in comfortably to my first-class seat, nails still in-tact, and tracks still tight. But the trip home was a little different this time. I felt lighter, almost as if a 200-pound boulder had been lifted off of me. I touched the home screen of my cracked phone screen and scrolled down until I reached the last text message I received from Rob in May of 2017, which I never responded to.

ROB: Are you ready to redeem yourself yet?

With one quick swipe to the left I deleted the message, along with the memory of the man I thought I knew and once loved. I laid my head back comfortably on the headrest and closed my eyes just in time to hear the voice over the loudspeaker announce, "flight attendants prepare for take-off."

Two Hennesseys, one coke, and one hell of a nap later, it was wheels down for me for what I hoped to be a while. All I wanted to do was kiss my kids, get my phone screen fixed, and take another nap.

EPILOGUE

To say that my life In *The Aftermath of R. Kelly* has been anything but perfect, is an understatement; however, I can honestly say that I am achieving peace and balance with each day that passes. After the airing of the first Lifetime docuseries *Surviving R. Kelly*, I received death threats and even experienced my first panic attack after a bomb scare during the December 2018 premiere. These incidents combined with the backlash I received from the public on social media, YouTube, and the blogs, was enough to send me over the edge and what ultimately led to my depression. The worst part is that many of those who attacked me were not only people from my past, but also from those that were once the closest to me like friends, family, and former lovers. They dug up every piece of dirt they could find, in an effort to break me down and they almost succeeded.

It has taken me a long time to overcome the feelings of shame, guilt, and regret that came along with revealing some of the most intimate aspects of my relationship with Rob (R. Kelly) to the world. I've also had to overcome the feelings of disappointment and sometimes rage, over the treatment and lack of support that I and others received from Lifetime and the media, especially the Black media. While I appreciate the opportunities that resulted from the Lifetime docuseries, I feel that the network unfairly profited from our pain and fell short when it came to providing the help we were promised. Help in the form of therapy and overall emotional and mental health support. And although a lot of the division that now exists between all of the "R. Kelly girls" started a long time ago, I personally feel that the network compounded it by secretly turning us against one another.

RECLAIMING MY POWER

One of my biggest regrets was and still is, not forming better and stronger bonds and alliances with the other girls who are also survivors. I truly believe that we could have been a hell of a lot better and stronger together, than apart. Unfortunately, since our collective "coming out" we have all gone our separate ways and now seem to be in competition with each other. Sometimes I feel as if I entered a competition that I didn't sign up for. Truth be told, I am really only competing with myself these days. But at the end of the day, I am still hopeful that we can somehow come together on some level or on some great platform that will prevent other young, black women from enduring the pain and shame that we did. But for now, I have set my intentions on continuing to speak my truth, rebuilding my brand, and inspiring others along the way.

Since the airing of the second piece, *Surviving R. Kelly, Part II - The Reckoning*, I am happy to say that the attacks have been fewer and far between and surprisingly, I've received more love than scrutiny this time around. In fact, things for me are finally starting to look up now that people have seen a glimpse into my life and the positive changes I've made in order to move forward. No longer am I a victim, but instead I'm a survivor, a victor, and an overcomer! My focus and intention has been set on raising my family, growing my HVAC business, and building my non-profit 501(c)(3) which I affectionately named after my three children. My children are who inspire me to do all that I do and be all that I can be. It's called G.A.S., The Fuel Behind The Fire and its mission and purpose is to help young women and men in domestic abuse situations, by providing them with counseling services, housing, and other assistance. As part of our mission, I want to help mentor and guide these individuals to make better choices in life and to reassure them that whatever their situation may be – that it is only temporary and that they are not to blame. I think far too often whenever we are in toxic or abusive situations, we tend to blame ourselves, like I once did. My goal is to stop that cycle with other young people who may experience what I did and even worse.

Some have asked if I will ever do another docuseries, given that the situation with Rob is far from over, with his trial quickly approaching. The answer is NO! I have vowed to never subject myself to that type of exploitation and humiliation again! Don't get me wrong, I am grateful for the opportunities that have arisen as a result; especially as a little black girl from New Orleans who would have never likely attended the Emmy's or MTV Awards, or appeared on such shows as Dateline, Megyn Kelly, and Dr. Oz. So for that part, I am very grateful.

As far as my personal life is concerned; as much as I wish I could say that I've found my love and that I've finally found my prince, I cannot. Instead, I've kissed a few other "frogs" since my split with Rob and have become more guarded about who I choose to trust and reveal myself with and open my heart to. I have chosen now to recognize and react upon the red flags instead of ignoring them and to seek my instinct and God's discernment in all of my relationships while trying to keep an open mind.

I've been asked and often asked myself, what I would say to Rob if our paths were to ever cross again. And while I have no desire to ever see or speak to him again; if given the chance, I would simply ask him *why? Why would you choose to treat me and other women in your life the way that you have when you professed to love us so much? That's not love.* More importantly, I would want him to admit that he is a sick man that needs help and to commit to getting the help that he needs. Mental illness is real. I witnessed it with my own biological mother and others in my life.

As for my mother, I still haven't spoken to her since 2014. But as much as I would like to forgive, reconcile and have a *real* relationship with her and the rest of my family, I have come to accept the fact that it may never happen. But if given the opportunity, I would pose the same question to her – *why? Why did you hate me so much? What did I ever do to you to make you treat me and your grandkids the way you have?* The hardest part of the whole ordeal with Rob has been facing my critics and own personal demons without the love and support of my own family. It's been hard, but I'm thankful for the love of strangers who have become like family to me and for those who have embraced and loved and supported me in my journey on the road to redemption.

As for the members of the Black media who I have oftentimes found to be my worst critics, I would urge them to stop the cycle and disrespect before it kills somebody, by causing someone to take his or her own life. I think author and radio host Charlemagne the God said it best when he said that "the most disrespected woman in America is the black women…If you want to get away w/sexual assault, assault a young black girl." I have found so often since my ordeal that the Black media underestimates our worth as black women and have implanted the myth that everything I and the others did has been about money and the fame, when that couldn't be the furthest from the truth. Why would anyone want to risk their families or their own lives for that?

And like Tarana Burke, the founder of the "Me Too" movement has said time and time again, "Black girls don't matter enough…" For me, it's time to change that narrative and time for Black women to stand up and stand together, instead of trying to stand on one another. It's time to reclaim our collective power and help each other to succeed. When that happens, we all win. Thank you for allowing me to share my story and I truly hope my journey has inspired you to be better, in some way.

~Asante~

ACKNOWLEDGEMENTS

I First and foremost, I would like to thank **my Lord & Savior Jesus Christ** for being my ROCK and for NEVER giving up on me like so many others in my life have. I owe you everything and will continue to seek your guidance and favor in everything I do. Thanks to you, I now have hope and believe in second chances again.

Thank you to **my kids** for always pushing me and for giving me a reason to continue to speak up and speak out. As much as I wish I could name you individually, as your mother, my job is to protect you, but you know who you are and the special place each of you holds in my life. You guys have given me courage to tell my truth and because of you guys, I never gave up on life and my purpose. My goal has and will always be to protect all of you and to make sure that you never end up in a toxic relationship(s) like I was. I love you with all of my heart and hope I have made you proud.

To **Ms. Terry Brazley**, thank you for always inspiring me to keep my head up, to ignore the naysayers and to believe that God can get me through anything and everything, which He has! Your friendship has helped me to hold steadfast to my faith. You have been the mother I never had. I love and thank you for your unconditional love.

To **Dr. Pullum and Taylor**, thank you both for not giving up on me even, when at times, I wanted to give up on myself. You knew my purpose and encouraged me to tell my story and share my testimony. Thank you for helping me to realize that life is so much bigger than Rob. And to the entire **PullCorp team**, thank you for the long nights and for dealing with the drama that I can often bring. I appreciate your positivity and ensuring that I remained positive and for your creativity in developing my brand and vision.

To **Schacle Powell**, thank you for always keeping my hair slayed for every event and for always pushing me to keep going and to "ignore the trolls," as you would say. I appreciate you more than words can express.

To author **Angie Ransome-Jones**, thank you for your expertise in transforming my innermost thoughts and secrets into a book that has brought my story to life. I thank you for not just listening to me, but for actually *hearing* me and everything I've experienced in my life. You coming to New Orleans to experience my world and seeing the places I grew up meant a lot to me. I appreciate you!

To my best friend, **Kenya "Smithy" Smith**, thank you for never judging me and for always being that ear that listened whenever I needed someone to share with, without judgement. Not once did you ever complain about my complaining. I love you for that and so much more!

ABOUT THE AUTHOR

A native of New Orleans, Louisiana; Asante McGee is a mother, entrepreneur, author, and a survivor. She was born into abuse, survived an 11-year abusive marriage, and most recently escaped from a two-year mentally abusive relationship with R&B sensation R. Kelly.

As a result of the long-term abuse she suffered, McGee thought abuse equaled love for many years. Since that time, however, she has learned to love herself and to show others love in the process. Through her growth, McGee has become a "voice for the voiceless" by speaking out about the abuse she suffered not only in the media, but in her first published book, *No Longer Trapped In The Closet, The Asante McGee Story* (2018) and most recently in her latest release entitled, *Reclaiming My Power, My Life in the Aftermath of R. Kelly (2020)*. McGee has also become an advocate for the abused. Most recently she founded a non-profit organization called G.A.S., The Fuel Behind The Fire, with the mission of assisting young women and men in domestic abuse situations through the provision of counseling services, housing, and other assistance.

When she is not traveling the country, speaking and advocating on behalf of victims of abuse, McGee manages one of Atlanta's most successful Heating, Ventilation, and Air Conditioning (HVAC) businesses, which she has proudly owned since 2017. McGee is best known for her appearances on both Lifetime docuseries entitled *Surviving R. Kelly and Surviving R. Kelly Part II – The Reckoning*. In addition, she has appeared on Dateline NBC, the Megyn Kelly show, Tom Joyner Morning Show, and has spoken at such renown national events as Essence Festival and the Black Authors and Readers Rock (BARR) book event.

McGee currently lives in the Atlanta Metropolitan area with her three loving children and grandson

www.ingramcontent.com/pod-product-compliance
Lightning Source LLC
Chambersburg PA
CBHW070935160426
43193CB00011B/1695